*Chapter 1
emunulate
noble
ex: Building trusting
relationships 3
Expressing compassion +
love

Don't Look Too Closely:

What Children of Trauma are Hiding & How You Can Be the Difference for Them

*Send CASA webnair
* send neuro emails
* Dr Perry??

* School accomodations,
    regarding regulation
*Like how you mention
several traumas, medical,
    neglect, etc. home life
* "End of the day takeaways are
    all spot on + great!

Don't Look Too Closely:

What Children of Trauma are Hiding & How You Can Be the Difference for Them

Belinda Adams

Anchor Book Press · Palatine

Don't Look Too Closely: What Children of Trauma are Hiding & How You Can Be the Difference for Them

Copyright © 2018 Belinda Adams
ISBN: 978-1-949109-00-9
Printed in the United States

Dedication

I would like to dedicate this book to my students. You stuck with me through my failures and our successes together! Yes, I realize that you have to go to school, but I appreciate your tolerance, acceptance, and respect.

Sorry it took me so long to realize it's a team effort, and we've got to be in the "race" together.

I wish all of you, success and happiness in the years ahead!

Acknowledgement

I'd like to acknowledge Mary, my Professor and Advisor at Judson University, who taught me that a person can make all the plans they want for their life, but don't get too attached to them, because you never know what plan God has for you.

I'd also like to acknowledge my fellow educators, many of whom put their lives in danger every day, in schools where violence is common.

You are true heroes to me!

Children of trauma demonstrate unique character traits in the classroom, traits which are often misinterpreted by unknowing teachers.

"Such characteristics can both negatively impact the educational experiences of traumatized students and present significant challenges for the teachers tasked with supporting them.

However, these same teachers are in a unique position to create a compassionate, encouraging environment for these students which ultimately improves the learning environment for everyone."

(Cevasco, NEA, Best Practices, 2002-2017).

Forward

I am so excited that you have chosen to read *Don't Look Too Closely*. In this book, Belinda Adams takes a look at hurting children. She shares her perspective with stories from her classroom, that help us to see what we can do to provide a bright spot in the lives of children who have experienced trauma.

The strategies in this book are not new and expensive, most require just a little of your time. However, they are not as easy as rocket science where 2 + 3 always equals 5. No, when we start talking about things to help students who have experienced trauma, we can't simply say here is the answer, because all children are different. As Belinda reminds us, 'one-size' does not fit all. It doesn't fit all teachers and it most certainly does not fit all students. Through years of tears and struggling to find answers, Belinda shares an assortment of strategies that we can tailor to our own teaching styles and to the unique problems and challenges our students face. If one strategy does not work, try another strategy or a combination of strategies.

Belinda is one of the most caring teachers I know. She has a passion for children who need someone to be there for them. She is continually looking for ways to make the classroom a place where students, all students, feel safe as she employs many strategies to help them be emotionally available to learn while imparting a sense of high expectations for students. Belinda has one of the highest success rates with difficult students – success rates measured in improved behavior **and** academic performance.

Now, some may glance through this book and feel that the strategies are not really that big of a deal. I'm here to say that they are. As a child of trauma myself, I can remember the overriding question of my childhood: Where are the people who are supposed to protect me? Growing up in a different time with less understanding of the impact of emotions on achievement, some years there was no one, but eventually, school became my place of refuge. The best teachers, I still remember – Mr. Daniels, Ms. Avery, Mrs. White. I excelled in their classes as I felt safe, protected, cared for. Looking back, no one did anything spectacular. Some just noticed my strengths, others always had a kind word or an encouraging comment when I needed to do better. Mostly, they cared and had confidence in my ability to succeed even though I could be difficult and I was not always on-task. These things were important, because school was the only place this was occurring during one particularly traumatic period of my life.

As I thought about *Don't Look Too Closely,* I remembered the feeling. Like the children in Belinda's class, I was hiding something. As a child, it can be embarrassing to admit the trauma you face daily. I only wanted to be loved and accepted, a normal kid – not the object of someone's pity. For pity, at least to me, suggested hopelessness. I wanted teachers and other adults to look beyond my situation, understanding life was difficult while they brought hope that life wouldn't always be that way. I needed role models to show me caring adults existed, especially when the people who cared for me had been ripped from my life. I yearned for someone to know me and know what I was capable of if I could just control the untamed emotional roller coaster driven by constant trauma.

Belinda tells us how we can do that for the students in our classroom. It does matter.

Belinda shows us some things we can do to help, but she is honest. Sometimes, the needs of students are beyond the ability of any one person to fulfill. Even in those cases, Belinda demonstrates ways we can provide some relief to a suffering child. I've known Belinda for many years and I can say this is more than just a job to her. When Belinda describes a child's story, she is talking about a child who has touched her heart and she has done all she could to help that child. While some stories do not have what we would consider happy endings, I am proof that we may not be looking at the ending. Today, I am a successful professional and I am able to talk about traumatic situations in my life objectively while remaining emotionally stable. However, if you had looked at my life in high school, you would not have thought the efforts of my teachers and other adults made any difference, but some situations require time for efforts to produce success. Don't discount your efforts because you are not privileged to see the difference you made in a child's life. Be thankful for the relief you were able to provide for a short time and hopeful that you aren't seeing the end.

Belinda seems to have a soft spot for hurting kids and a radar for students of trauma. *Don't Look Too Closely,* shows strategies she uses to help students feel accepted, worthy, and empowered to learn. As Belinda says, "We must challenge ourselves to see their pain while still encouraging them to learn." We have a choice. Some may say, this is not my job and choose not to get involved. I hope that through the words of this book, you will be inspired to choose to help students, especially hurting students. Belinda wrote this book to share her strategies, if you find them helpful let others know about the book. If we all choose to step up, everyone benefits – the students, the teachers, and even society. Will you be the difference for the hurting kids in your life?

Annie -Childhood Trauma Survivor

Table of Contents

Defining Trauma

I'll be candid in admitting that before I became an educator, and for a few years after I became an educator, I thought of "trauma" as the aftermath of the dramatic scenes depicted on television shows like *ER* or *911*.

You know what I'm envisioning, right? Graphic images of entire homes burning down. Families destroyed by murder or fatal accidents. My mind would sweep through news stories where traumatic events are described in universal ways, but where few fail to mention the individuals of the tragedy being reported.

While it seems, there are many books about helping children deal with the trauma of divorce or helping your child deal with the trauma of childhood disease, few books address the "everyday" trauma, the trauma that some children live with day in and day out, the effects of which they bring into our classrooms. How do we address the trauma we can't see or the forgotten trauma?

It took a few pointed lessons, or should I call them, instructional disasters, before I realized there were victims of trauma sitting in the seats of my classroom. It became apparent to me that I needed to understand trauma and its effects if I was ever going to be able to "get through to them".

According to the National Institute of Mental Health, childhood trauma is defined as: "The experience of an event by a child that is emotionally painful or distressful, which often results in lasting mental and physical effects"

(Illinois Department of Human Resources, http://lookthroughtheireyes.org/what-is-childhood-trauma/).

Further, the Illinois Department of Human Resources lists the following as the most common causes of childhood trauma:

- Serious accidents;
- Bullying/cyberbullying;
- Chaos or dysfunction in the house (including parent with a mental illness, substance

abuse, domestic violence, or parent that is incarcerated);

- Death of a loved one;
- Emotional abuse or neglect;
- Physical abuse or neglect;
- Separation from a parent or caregiver;
- Sexual abuse;
- Stress caused by poverty; and
- Sudden and/or serious medical condition.

As educators, if we dismissively think every child in our classrooms has escaped all traumatic events, we're kidding ourselves or hiding our heads in the sand. The National Child Traumatic Stress Network reports that "One out of every 4 children attending school has been exposed to a traumatic event that can affect learning and/or behavior" (Trauma Facts for Teachers, NCTSC, 2008).

Most of us know someone who has gone through at least one of the traumatic events listed previously. We know people who have experienced trauma and seemingly come out unscathed, both emotionally and physically. Others we know seem "stuck" in their trauma, unable to move forward and incapable of experiencing the joys of a normal life.

When these individuals are adults, we encourage them to Google their symptoms, seek resources, and look for a good psychologist and support group. However, experiencing trauma becomes even more incapacitating, answers more elusive, when the individual experiencing trauma is a child.

Trauma Hiding in the Classroom

As a teacher of many grades over the course of my career, it's safe to say that I've encountered my fair share of challenging students.

In my first-grade classroom, they were the sullen ones that you felt exceptionally blessed if you could get a smile out of them. Or the petulant ones who seemed to pout over everything and it appeared nothing you planned would make them happy. Or the defiant ones who crawled under desks and chairs, refusing to participate or do anything being requested of them.

In my 5th grade, special education classroom, the challenging students were, what's the word, taller! And therefore, a little more intimidating. There were those who defied me with their eyes and showed mistrust of any efforts on my part to build rapport. There were those who taunted me with verbal assaults and comments meant to wound me or derail whatever it was I was teaching. There were those who confronted me physically, turning over chairs and desks and slamming doors in anger. Lastly, there were those students who seemed to retreat into themselves, appearing to be living their dream of becoming invisible.

After a few years of teaching, my husband and son pointed out that it was those same challenging students that threatened my sanity and often drove me to tears of frustration at the onset of the school year, were the students who became my "favorite" students by the end of the school year. And they were correct, although I am at a loss to explain how that happened. But year after year, it did!

As I've thought about these "challenging" students preparing to write this book, I recalled many details about their home lives and realized that, whether I knew about it at the time or not, the majority of my challenging students were victims of some form of trauma, whether it was poverty, drug or alcohol abuse in the home, domestic violence, illness, or death of a loved one. It was still trauma.

Throughout this book, you'll read notes from parents and students I've kept over the years. Some notes bring smiles of remembrance about a particular student's quirkiness while other notes bring sadness when I recall that not all of my classroom stories conclude with happy endings. Nope, teaching isn't like a Disney movie where everything wraps up in a tidy little bow at the end of the year.

I've kept the notes, regardless of the emotions they evoke, to remind myself of the powerful impact I have as a teacher on young minds. I don't want to forget that, not for one single day. Because a good relationship with a teacher might be the only positive relationship that child has in his or her life!

The stories in this book are really *their* stories! The trauma they faced that resulted in the challenging behavior in my classroom became a part of me as I tried to discover how I could support them, reassure them, and instruct them in the mere 6 hours a day I called them "mine."

Because the stories are real stories and the children are real children, some details have been changed to protect their privacy and prevent others from identifying any particular child. I have not changed the trauma, the circumstances, and the affect they had on my students.

"We must consider how disordered emotions and

behavior look and feel from the perspective

of the child or youth.

Our conceptualizations cannot be complete

until we have been able to set aside the analysis

of 'problem' or 'disorder' from the

adult's perspective and see it through the child's
eyes"

(Kauffman, 205, p. 45-46).

Belinda Adams

Role of the Teacher & Trauma

My first principal once told me his view of teaching. Being that he'd been in the teaching business for over 30 years, I took it to heart that his words held value. He told me that successful teachers are those who accept the "gifts" that each child brings to the table (our classroom). He said that we (educators) shouldn't spend time and energy wishing they had gifts they don't have. It's frustrating for the teacher and debilitating for the child. He ended by saying that it is caring teachers who give kids the feeling that they are accepted, make them feel worthy, and empower them to learn (Craig Sundstedt, 2003).

After years in the classroom myself, I still believe the value of his statements and try to embrace them each year with whichever students are assigned to my roster. As a parent, I know firsthand how much I respected my son's teachers who saw him for the "gem" he was, and I watched him grow emotionally and academically under their caring efforts. I try to find the "gem" in each of my students.

Karen Dockery in her book entitled, *When a Hug Won't Fix the Hurt*, writes about the critical need for teachers who understand how trauma impacts children. She describes the teachers who are prepared to do what it takes to help them feel safe and secure in the learning environment.

She writes to parents: "Foundational to working as a team is choosing the right teacher in the first place. The teacher who works with your child daily helps him walk through his challenges and interprets the crisis to friends. Some teachers are better at this close contact and compassionate caring than others" (Dockery, 2000, p. 135).

She continues by saying, "A teacher may see special needs as a bother, communicating this resentment to your child and causing your child to wonder why his teacher doesn't like him. Seek the critical balance between modification and high expectation, between compassion and discipline, between taking the crisis seriously and overreacting" (Dockery, 2000, p. 135).

I want to draw attention to a critical concept in her words that is commonly overlooked by educators and parents. Dockery points out the importance of finding that balance between "compassion and discipline." Too often, I hear teachers talking about traumatic events a student might be facing and they usually finish the story with, "I feel so sorry for her and I'm not sure how to help."

As callous as it might sound, feeling sorry for a student accomplishes nothing and often leaves them stuck right where they are. To be sure, it is critical, as an educator, that our actions speak of empathy for the student, and yet they must also communicate a level of expectation about school work. Merriam-Webster defines empathy as "the action of being understood, being aware, being sensitive to, and vicariously experiencing the feelings of another". We must challenge ourselves to see their pain while still encouraging them to learn.

In her book, *Children and Trauma*, Monahon states the importance of relationship: "The task of coping for children who lack at least one person who can understand and comfort them in their pain is understandably so difficult that the defense of a quick burial makes total but tragic sense. Just one person who recognizes and responds to the child's pain, one person who can help the child look in the face of terror, can make an enormous difference" (1995, p. 179).

I believe that, if we as educators, choose to focus on two questions posed in an National Education Association (NEA) article and let the latter question drive our instruction in the classroom where trauma affects students, it would make a world of difference. Rather than asking, "What's wrong with you?" let's ask "What's happened to you?" (Cevasco, NEA, Best Practices, 2002-2017).

Once we can begin to understand what has happened to the children we are attempting to educate, we can begin the process of developing a rapport that leads to learning.

After years of experiencing struggles, failures and successes at developing student/teacher rapport, I strongly believe that, once a student knows you care, they care what you have to teach them!   CASA

"*I hire teachers with one specific characteristic.*

I hire teachers who care about kids.

I can teach teachers to teach,

but I cannot teach them to care."

(Retired Principal,
Craig Sundstedt,
2003)

Belinda Adams

Where to Begin?

I would be untruthful if I didn't admit that there have been times when I've come home from school after the first day of meeting my new students and thought about how appealing that job as a Barista at Starbucks was looking. Usually, I was put off by what appeared to be a lack of interest or excitement about learning from my students that seemed almost appalling, not to mention overwhelming.

I've often wondered, where do I start? First and foremost, I've learned that I've got to get to know those students! I need to know what interests them and what frightens them. I've got to know *who* they are before I can begin to teach them. This was not new information. I'd heard it many times, but never implemented it thoroughly enough to be helpful. I've discovered it isn't enough to know how many siblings they have or their favorite color. I've got to dig deeper!

At the onset, understanding the unique needs of students of trauma seems like a huge task, indeed. However, as experts have stated again and again, the strategies a teacher implements to assist students of trauma are strategies that will positively impact all students in the classroom! That's a relief to me, knowing that I didn't need to identify those students of trauma the first week of school, and it should be encouraging to all teachers as well.

As educators, we shouldn't be afraid to step outside of our comfort zone to establish relationships and build rapport with all students. The NEA's article on Best Practices suggests that teachers begin with a "trauma-informed approach to education". What does this look like? "The trauma-informed approach to education aims to implement techniques that benefit students with trauma histories, educators, and the larger educational community as a whole."

" ...Most importantly, a trauma-informed approach abandons the notion that punitive discipline or special education referrals are a frontline intervention when symptoms emerge.

Rather, such an approach encourages educators to ask, 'What's happened to you?' instead of 'What's wrong with you?'" (Cevasco, NEA, Best Practices, 2002-2017). ←ASA

And surely, those of us who have faced those difficult students in our classroom, while at the same time looking into the apt, smiling faces of other students, find it sometimes impossible to keep ourselves from asking, either aloud or in our thoughts, "What *is* wrong with that kid?" Sadly, I must admit that I've still asked the question, either to myself or a colleague. Unfortunately, I've realized, even knowing the answer to the question usually doesn't solve the issues the student poses in my classroom nor does it provide me with specific ideas on how to help that student become a successful learner.

Kauffman states, "Surprises are part of teaching children with emotional or behavioral disorders, even after one has been at it for many years. Mistakes and disappointments, as well as successes and gratification, are part of the territory" (2005, p. 45-46).

In her words, I've found comfort and resolve to keep trying, in knowing that I won't always get it right.

~End of the Day Takeaways~

When asking where to start making sense of what I was seeing in the class, I found myself sitting with one of my old college textbooks. In one of the margins, I read a very pointed question:

Are you a reflective teacher? I'd written.

According to the text, it said a reflective teacher is "thoughtful and inventive. Reflective teachers think back over situations to analyze what they did and why they did it to consider how they might improve learning for students."

(Woolfolk, p. 7, 2001)

Sometimes, I must admit that I am a bit too reflective, and "beat up" myself for classroom scenarios that veered radically from where I intended them to go. I've learned that I have to remind myself, as I do my students, that I am human, and capable of mistakes and there's always tomorrow to try again.

Acceptance

Belinda Adams

Trauma & the Young Mind

Without question, I believe seeing young children who have been affected by trauma is probably the most heartbreaking and difficult for us, as educators, to deal with on a daily basis. If we are parents ourselves, I believe it's even harder as we can't help but think about what we might do if our child was experiencing a similar issue. At times, it's difficult not to grab them up in our arms to comfort them and look for ways (perhaps beyond the scope of our jobs) to help them get over the pain they may be experiencing.

I recall students whose sadness all day made it extremely difficult for me to watch them head home each evening. This was especially true if I was aware that they might be going home to experience further trauma or if I knew they would not find comfort from the ones they most desired it from, their parents and family!

As their teachers, we see them for a mere 6 urs a day and have only so much control over how we can help them deal with their trauma. Especially when it's also our job to educate them at the same time!

In the book, *Ghosts from the Nursery*, the authors describe the debilitating effects of young childhood trauma: "When the brain is first formed, both the quantity and quality of tissue and chemistry can be changed by the sensitization to trauma. The same experiences can change the brain of an older child, also, but in the beginning, in infancy and toddlerhood, while it is at its most malleable, the brain actually organizes itself around these conditions. ...And attention and capacities in the brain originally available for learning other skills may be deflected to help defend against future trauma" (Karr-Morse & Wiley, 1997, p. 159).

Chronic exposure to traumatic events, especially during a child's early years, can:

- Adversely affect attention, memory, and cognition.
- Reduce a child's ability to focus, organize, and process information.

* fight or flight
* strong supports w/ this
+ Neurofeedback on campus

- Interfere with effective problem solving and/or planning.
- Result in overwhelming feelings of frustration and anxiety" (The National Child Traumatic Stress Network (NCTSN), 2008, p. 5).

Further, the NCTSN warns teachers of the dangers of students who demonstrate other, specific behaviors. They advise educators, "Be alert to the behavior of the students who have experienced one or more of these events. Be aware of both the children who act out AND the quiet children who don't appear to have behavioral problems. These students often "fly beneath the radar" and do not get help. They may have symptoms of avoidance and depression that are just as serious as those of the acting out student" (NCTSN, 2008, p. 9).

As you read the stories of my 1st and 2nd grade students, it is my hope that you find a new lens in which to view your students and their actions. In that way, you might see yourself in my successes and failures, and discover your own strategies that might provide these children with hope for a better future.

Perhaps, with all of our efforts, we can help these children visualize and act towards a future without the fear of additional trauma and a future with dreams that their life situations will improve!

THEIR STORIES

Belinda Adams

Preferential Practices

JOEY: Just Watching TV

While I've met many lovable and charming students since beginning teaching, I have to admit that there has been only one student that I emphatically said, "I'd bring that little boy home and raise him." This statement was absorbed with dismay and an "I hope she never really asks me to do that," expression on my husband's face.

This little boy was named Joey and he was in my first-grade class. He was a student who, without really even trying, made my job of teaching him more difficult for a few reasons. He frequently missed school or was tardy at least 3 out of the 4 days he attended school; he didn't speak often and rarely responded with more than a one-word answer; he showed little to no emotion on his face (unless it was recess); and he hid under his desk every day when it was time for math because, in his own words, "Maff scares me!"

If you're an educator, you know how hindering frequent absences are, especially for the primary years when skills build a foundation like building blocks one upon the other with each passing day. And Joey, already behind in his 1st grade class due to missing more than half of his Kindergarten year, couldn't afford to miss school as often as he did. As I sadly learned, simply calling a parent and telling them about the importance of regular school attendance didn't necessarily change their habits of allowing frequent absenteeism.

Out of frustration for Joey's' situation, I went searching for information. I spoke to his Kindergarten teacher, the social worker, the principal, and anyone else who knew the family. With their help, I was able to piece together some facts about my little absentee boy.

Joey lived with his mother who spoke only Spanish and his father who spoke English and a little Spanish and his older brother who spoke both Spanish and English. His mother worked the night shift and his father worked the day shift, and neither shift was conducive to getting Joey to school on time. It was the responsibility of his high school brother to get himself up and get Joey to school each day. Not an easy task when the big brother's absenteeism was just as high as Joey's. A tenuous situation to be sure.

Working with Mom and Dad, the social worker and I came up with a possible solution to get Joey to school, even if he was late. His parents were stunned to hear that his first-grade teacher wasn't going to lecture about Joey being tardy for school. It seems they'd already heard enough lectures about tardiness during Joey's Kindergarten year. I answered, "Are you kidding? I want Joey at school each day, and I don't care if he doesn't get here until lunch; just get him here!"

With that understanding, Joey's attendance improved. When Mom got home from work, she would make sure that Joey and his brother were up for school and heading out the door (even though she arrived home after school had begun). Dad became part of the team too when he agreed to see that Joey was in bed at a decent hour to get enough sleep to be physically and emotionally available for learning the next day.

Even with this, the reality of Joey's situation didn't hit home for me until the day Joey was really late for school! I was concerned because they hadn't "called him in sick" and no one was answering the phone at his house. The liaison for the district was called and sent over to the house to check on the family. After knocking repeatedly and no one coming to the door, he took a quick peek through the window. To his surprise, he saw Joey sitting in front of the TV eating Cheerios out of the box. When he was finally able to get Joey's attention to come to the door to let him in, he discovered that Joey was home alone. You might ask: How did a 6-year-old end up home alone at 10 in the morning?

As the story was told to me, Mom left Dad a note the night before saying she would be working overtime the next morning and she would be unable to get Joey up for school. The father hadn't seen the message, had gone to bed, gotten up early for work, and left the house before 6 am. The brother hadn't come home the night before, having told his parents he was staying the night with a friend. They had forgotten.

When Joey woke up that morning, he got dressed and sat down in front of the TV to eat his cereal until someone told him it was time for school. Not being able to tell time, he didn't know it was 10 in the morning. Further, and more upsetting, was the awareness that he had so little interaction with his parents and brother, he didn't know he was home alone!

This knowledge saddened me; how had this family ended up in this situation? And how had this little boy become accustomed to so little communication with his family members that this situation seemed to have no impact on him whatsoever?

That day, I decided that someone had to be there for Joey, and it appeared it was going to have to be me. I became his defender that day. I held my tongue when he was late day after day, welcoming him with a smile and saying I was glad he was there. I asked the front office staff not to say anything about his tardiness to Joey or his family. I did additional planning that I thought might engage him in our instruction and did everything short of standing on my head to solicit a smile. And until "maff" no longer scared him, I passed him a lapboard with his math paper and pencil and he did his math under his desk. Little by little, a relationship of trust was built.

As the year progressed, with a little prompting and a big smile, I finally got him to come to the bulletin board when it was his turn to do calendar. With nods and two thumbs up that assured him I was sure he had the correct answer, I would sometimes elicit a response from him. He was showing signs of being the 6-year-old boy he deserved to be!

One morning, my husband who was a police officer working the night shift, called me on my way to school to tell me about a call he'd had the previous evening. While on duty, he'd overheard a call for police assistance in the neighborhood where Joey and his family lived. Recognizing the address and understanding my attachment to this little boy, my husband rushed over.

When my husband arrived, it was quite a scene: The brother was being arrested by Immigrations Customs Enforcement (ICE) after having been caught with a knife. When the officers began to handcuff the teenager, the mother rushed the officers, begging them not to take her boy. She too was placed in the squad car, under arrest for assaulting an officer.

As my husband took in the scene, he noticed Joey looking outside through the upstairs window. He asked about Joey's father and was told he was on the way, but they had a warrant for his arrest. My husband took another look at Joey's little face in the window and went to speak to the ICE officers. Quickly, he explained that Joey was a student of his wife's, and that Joey's mother was important to getting him to school and would soon be the only wage-earning adult in the home if Joey's father was going to be arrested. He ended, "And if that kid is left alone, I can guarantee you, he'll be living in my guest room tomorrow because my wife loves that little kid!" I was thankful to hear that when Joey's mother was released, she went silently into the house.

I've kept track of Joey over the years. When I saw him in a 5th grade classroom, he still had a cautious smile but came to school every day. He had friends and had learned to excel at academics, even "maff".

Kauffman echoes the positive effects of the instructional measures I took in the classroom by saying, "Preferential interventions by the teacher sometimes solve problems and avoid referral to special education" (Kauffman, 2005, p. 26).

Did I think, at the time, that providing Joey with a lapboard and his math paper and pencil under his desk was going to help him get past his fear of "maff"? Absolutely not! At the time, I was looking for a way to get this kid to do his math, while at the same time, avoiding a power struggle that rarely results in success for the child or the teacher.

Sometimes, what we do intuitively, as educators, to facilitate the process of learning using the path of least resistance is the best approach. One might even wonder if it is fair to give a child preferential treatment. I always remind myself, life is not a level playing field; certainly not for the Joeys of the world. Anytime it is within our power to do something for a child who is struggling, we should do it without hesitation.

Some might say what happened to Joey that day he was left alone is not a traumatic experience; just a mere miscommunication problem. That might be true in some cases. However, knowing what I know about the family situation, and Joey's complete disconnect from the incident, demonstrated what experts define as neglect.

well said

Paul Tough writes in Helping Children Succeed that a "growing body of evidence suggests that one of the most serious threats to a child's healthy development is neglect — the mere absence of responsiveness from a parent or caregiver" (Tough, 2016, p. 31). Joey's situation doesn't fall into the neglect definition that results in a threat to the child's physical wellbeing. Joey wasn't being abused, he had regular meals, etc. However, Tough describes a category of neglect called "chronic under stimulation, in which parents just don't interact very often with their children in an engaged, face-to-face, serve-and-return way, ignoring their cries or attempts at conversation, parking them in front of a screen for hours at a time" ough, 2016, p. 31). Even this level of neglect, according to Tough and study results, will result in "profound and lasting disruptive effect on the development of the brain" (Tough, 2016, p. 32).

In Joey's case, as a teacher, when I've gone searching for reasons a child is the way he is in order to help me better teach him, I've learned not to ignore the little stuff. Often, the little stuff can seem pretty big in the mind of a little person. In his book, Tough says children who have suffered chronic under stimulation "fall behind on measures of cognition and language development, and they have executive-function problems, too: They struggle with attention regulation; they are perceived by their teachers and parents as inattentive and hyperactive; they have trouble focusing in school" (Tough, 2016, p. 32).

Do you recognize the characteristics of Joey in any of the students you've had in your classrooms?

Developing Skills for Self-Expression

ROBERT: The World Outside

I had a little, red-haired boy named Robbie one year in my 1st grade class. He liked me to call him "Robert" because "that's what my Grandma calls me" and so I did. I recall him fondly because he liked to write notes for me and leave them on my desk at the end of the day where I'd find them after the students had gone home for the day. Learning to read 6-year-old phonetic spelling is quite a challenge, but after a while, it becomes pretty natural.

One such note read: "OBiN if you dar" Inside it said: "I luv you and I like sgool. Love Robert to Misis Adms".

I have his note to this day because, not only was I elated that he loved school, it was the first time he'd ever written anything remotely resembling words!

All of the teachers and staff knew about Robert's family because there were multiple siblings in several grades and one that had already moved on to middle school. Whenever calls were made home, it was Grandma who returned the calls or came to school for meetings. I'd often see the Grandmother walking the sidewalk with a basket full of laundry going from her home on one street to Robert's home on another street.

When curiosity finally got the best of me, I asked another teacher why Robert's mother never came to school and why the Grandmother was carrying laundry back and forth?

The teacher wasn't sure where to start with the story as she'd known the family since before the changes occurred. To simplify, it seems that Robert's mother stopped leaving the house when Robert's father up and left the family one day without a goodbye. Her depression resulted in her making fewer and fewer trips outside the home until she became an agoraphobic. She had not left the house for two years.

When I hear stories like this, I'm always amazed how the student functions in school at all. How could Robert look so normal and write such cute notes when his world was apparently upside down? But somehow, he did.

Robert did very well academically that year in 1st grade. He learned to read and write. Writing stories became a favorite activity for him. Writing, even using phonetic spelling, seemed to provide him with an outlet for sharing his ideas in a way that also left him feeling somewhat protected.

Whenever he'd write stories, he'd write about how he dreamed of the day his father would return and take him away with him to go cross country in the big rig he drove for a living. I was never really sure if that's what Robert's father did, or if that was just the story he'd been told. My heart ached for this little boy, who watched out his window for his father to appear.

At the beginning of Robert's 2nd grade year, my Principal dropped a note in my mailbox. It read: "I just watched Robbie choose words from the board and create a sentence, and then read the sentence to the class. It is hard to realize that one year ago, he did not recognize the letters in the alphabet. He is a success story! Congratulations on your work with Robbie."

If only that fantastic academic progress had continued. Unfortunately, that was not to be the case. In the 3rd grade, Robert started picking fights with other students. His frazzled Grandmother was at school daily, with no idea how to change the rising tides of misbehavior.

In the 5th grade, he was so out of control, it was recommended by his team of teachers and the special education department that he be placed in an outpatient therapeutic school, for the safety of himself and others. With this advice, his mother pulled him from school and decided to homeschool him.

I've never been quite certain what happened to Robert. I heard one story that he eventually ended up in an outpatient therapy school.

Another story told was that his father did, indeed, show up and take him cross country one summer before enrolling him in a military school for boys. However, like many of our students, there are so many questions that will remain unanswered.

An article in Psychology Today discussed the type of trauma Robert was experiencing, calling it emotional abandonment. According to the author,

Claudia Black, "emotional abandonment occurs when parents do not provide the emotional conditions and the emotional environment necessary for healthy development. I like to define emotional abandonment as 'occurring when a child has to hide a part of who he or she is in order to be accepted, or to not be rejected'" (Black, 2010).

After reading that article, I wondered again how Robert had come to school each day and functioned? Did he feel he needed to hide a part of himself in order to be accepted? Maybe, not consciously because he was so young; however, he certainly never shared why his mom didn't attend conferences or school performances.

Further, how Black describes what it means to "hide part of yourself" might go a long way towards explaining the actions of Robert in later grades. Often students use behavior to draw attention from other things. She explains that children experiencing this trauma often feel as though they cannot make mistakes, that sharing feelings is not allowed, and that their own needs are less important than the needs of others in the household, and because accomplishments are rarely, if ever, acknowledged, what's the point in *having successes?* (Black, 2010, https://www.psychologytoday.com/blog/the-many-faces-addiction/201006/understanding-the-pain-abandonment).

There's a part of me that wishes I'd had more information and strategies at the time to assist Robert in learning to live with the trauma in his life. However, last I checked, I don't have a time machine, and wishing doesn't change the facts. I rest myself in knowing that educating myself about trauma and its effects helped me be ready for future Roberts in my classroom.

~End of the Day Takeaways~

I'd like to think that Robert found happiness and normalcy in my classroom. I know with certainty that he found an outlet when he learned to write and could share his thoughts, feelings, and especially his hopes and dreams for a future. I know that Robert's story may not be one of celebration, as he struggled with his life choices after leaving my 1st grade class. Even if his life didn't appear to be headed in the right direction at that time, I want to think that the skills he learned and the acceptance he felt might be a foundation for his later success.

Jeffrey Benson in his book entitled, Hanging Ir Strategies for Teaching the Students that Challenge Us Most, writes about what I was witnessing with Robert, "Many young people do not have words for their feelings. They may be verbally limited to 'sad-mad-glad' but physically feel so much more. Students who have been traumatized, both at home and school, can be flooded with emotions and sensations-but not able to say what they are feeling" (2014, p.31).

Benson continues, "They react. When an adult can give the student a name for the feeling, the student can sometimes let go of the behavior, because someone has noticed" (2014, p. 31).

I KNOW that Robert felt "noticed" in my classroom, and his little notes demonstrated he was touched by our relationship. I try to remind myself when I struggle with a student's trauma that cannot be resolved in one year with efforts at school, that I have no control over that child's future. However, I DO have control over how that child feels about himself while he is my student. I can make that child feel welcome and safe, or I can look away, so I don't see the pain and ignore my responsibility. I choose to try to reach out, provide support, and teach every child that walks through my classroom door, regardless of the outcomes I may have experienced in the past. Each student deserves the best I have to give.

Belinda Adams

Being Present Day In/Day Out

MEGAN: Only 30 Days

Having a new student arrive mid school year is a very common occurrence when teaching in a low-income school. In fact, I've had students arrive, leave, and return during the same school year. It's very sad for me because it makes for such a difficult transition when life in the classroom has continued while they were gone, including development of peer relationships and academic growth. It's hard for students to "just pick up where they left off."

So, I wasn't surprised when, one morning the secretary appeared at my door with a little mouse of a girl and said she'd be starting in my class that day. Her name was Megan and she was very small for a 6-year-old. I recall thinking that she had the biggest brown eyes I'd ever seen! Probably why I noticed them was because they were also the saddest eyes I'd ever seen, especially on a little girl.

For the first few days, she said nothing; only nodding yes or no to questions as she moved about the classroom like a silent shadow. When it was time for classwork, instead of working she would lay across her desk and place her head in her arms. All attempts at trying to engage her were futile. I called home to speak to the parent, or at least, that's who I thought I was calling.

When I called the number listed in her contacts, I was told I was speaking to her Aunt. I explained my concerns about Megan and asked how I might be able to help her open up and be successful in learning. The conversation that followed reminded me of all of the things they don't teach you in college. Few experiences in my life had prepared me to deal with the story the Aunt told me.

She explained that Megan and her little brother, who was three, had come to live with them because their mother, her sister, was in court-mandated alcohol treatment. The children were removed from her custody by state authorities when neighbors had called about concerns of neglect. The young children, who were now living in a car with their mother, were taken into protective custody and then placed with the Aunt and Uncle.

The Aunt further explained that Megan had been unresponsive since arriving to their home, seemingly too traumatized to engage in conversation of any kind. I thanked the Aunt for the information and assured her I would do my best to make Megan feel at home in my classroom.

Armed with this new knowledge, I began a campaign of exceptional warmth when talking with Megan. I used a quiet voice, squatted down next to her to talk, and made sure I was aware of any changes in her facial expressions that might indicate anxiety or fear. If I sensed anything, I'd take a few extra minutes to check in with her to ask how I might help her do her work. I also enlisted the assistance of the social worker to help Megan open up.

I'll never forget the first words she said to me. Lifting her head from the desk, she whispered, "It's only 25 more days" and put her head back down on her desk. When I called the Aunt later that day to tell her of Megan's comment, the Aunt explained that Megan had been told her Mom was in a 30-day treatment program. Despite the neglect, Megan was counting down the days until she was back with her mom.

My heart was breaking for this little girl! Did she really plan to lay on the desk for the entire 30 days? How could I reach her? Engage her?

Little by little, with the help of the social worker, Megan came out of the shadows to join the class. She loved read-aloud time after lunch, and I was heartened when I saw a sparkle in her eye (however brief) when I read a story about a mischievous puppy or outlandish character. She enjoyed watching the others play at recess each day, although she rarely left my side.

As the 30-day mark approached, she began to become more and more animated, and I started to wish I'd be able to keep Megan in my classroom a bit longer. Maybe I shouldn't have thought that notion because, much to Megan's sadness, her mother was not released after the 30 days due to breaking the rules at the alcohol rehabilitation facility. When Megan learned the news, she returned to her despondent state.

As 30 days turned into three months, Megan slowly began to become part of the class. With much coaxing, she started playing at recess and seemed to enjoy the structure and safety in the home of her Aunt and Uncle. Most of all, she smiled occasionally, and when I was able to get a small giggle to erupt unexpectantly from her, it seemed the sun rose in the classroom, if only for a moment. Most of all, her big brown eyes didn't always look so sad. It was wonderful to watch the little steps of progress she was making each week.

Then, more change for Megan. During the fourth month, Megan's Aunt called to say that the father had found his way to Illinois, learned the circumstances of his children, and had gone to court for custody of the children. I was told that little Megan would be leaving that night, going to live with her father in Michigan. Sadly, I never got to say goodbye to Megan.

I've often wondered about Megan, and her response to such traumatic events. Thinking of myself in the same situation, I couldn't imagine her desire to be back with her mother, especially under the conditions in which she was found. However, understanding it or not, that's what this little girl was yearning for ... her mother.

While researching, I was dismayed to over that 26.8 million children are exposed to alcohol or drug dependency in the home, according to The US National Council on Alcohol and Drug Dependency reports (2015).

Although Megan might be a number in those statistics, and her symptoms detailed in articles, Megan was more than a statistic for me. Watching that little girl wait for 30 days to pass, and then, conversely, to see the positive changes that occurred once she was provided with normalcy in her life was terrific, and heartbreaking.

Dockery writes, "Children's honesty makes it both easier and more heart wrenching to encounter crises with them. No matter how agonizing the words, accept the child's feelings and your feelings in order to really heal. Denying feelings or holding them in causes a festering wound" (Dockery, 2000 p. 20).

acceptance

When I think about Megan, I hope that the time in my classroom provided her with a haven from her sadness, however brief it might have been. I also hope that the relationship we developed showed Megan the possibilities of positive relationships in the class and she was able to make a smooth transition to her new school and life with her Dad.

A few weeks after she'd gone, I received a note in my mailbox at school. It read:

"Mrs. Adams, You are truly a rare thing these days! It's nice to know a teacher can still care and put forth a little 'extra'. Thanks for everything, Megan's Aunt and Uncle."

Next was a note from Megan that read: "Mrs. Adams, Thank you for caring about me, Love Megan" and finally a quick note from her dad reading, "Thank you so much for everything you have done! You seem to be a wonderful caring teacher. I wish there were more teachers like you out there.   Thanks, Megan's daddy."

Creating Positive Memories

JAYDEN: What would she think?

My first year teaching I had a small classroom in a low-income school teaming with 34 wiggly, first-graders, mostly Hispanic, a handful of African Americans, including one curly-haired nymph of a little boy. To say I learned many lessons that year would be a complete understatement of the situation.

Imagine my elation when, over 10 years later, I received an email from that curly-haired little nymph who had just graduated from high school? "Mrs. Adams" he wrote, "I've never forgotten you and the way you used to make us laugh and all the things you did just to get us to read a book and do our math. I'd love to see you and tell you all about the things I've done. I'm off to college in the fall. I just wanted you to know that. Do you think we could meet?"

Well, after I'd stopped crying, I quickly sent back an email with my phone number and said "Give me a call. I'd love to see you!"

On a beautiful summer day, I found myself waiting impatiently outside of a coffee shop, wondering if I'd recognize him after so many years. As I searched the faces of the people walking towards me, I caught a glimpse of bobbing, curly hair, and instantly, I knew it must be him!

Amazed, I listened to Jayden's story of all the events he'd experienced after being removed from his mother's care to live with his grandmother. He talked about his struggles to find a balance between loving a mom who hadn't been there for him and wanting to make his grandmother proud. I smiled. And he said, "What? I know you're thinking something ..." I said, "Oh, kiddo, I'm sure you make your grandma proud every day. Just look at you!" He'd smiled and said, "You always used to say things like that!" Had I? I didn't remember. What I remembered was being a frazzled first year teacher with squirrelly students who seemed to find a million ways to test my patience. So, I asked him what he remembered most about that year. Well, to hear him tell it, he remembered every day!

He remembered our daily "Hokey Pokey" before lunch, the read-alouds after lunch to a bunch of kids who had never heard a story read aloud before, and our daily afternoon release to "Who Let the Dogs Out?" He laughed and said, "I'm pretty sure we were the only class in the whole school who left every day barking!" Well, he's probably right about that!

He talked about how he'd often wondered aloud, "I wonder what Mrs. Adams' would say?" as he pondered life's questions. He said he felt I had been with him all those years.

I was so proud of the young man Jayden had become. He was insightful, caring, and loving. I listened carefully as he spoke about his plans for the fall of starting at a local community college and working part-time. "I'd like to help my Grandma out with the bills, you know?", he said, "especially after all she did for me." I'd thought to myself how rare it is to find a young man of eighteen with such a sense of loyalty and responsibility.

When I first saw Jayden's next email arrive with the heading "college," my thoughts spun ahead to tales of how much he was learning. No, that wasn't the case. It seemed that Jayden was having a difficult time balancing the responsibilities of attending college and holding down a full-time job, and his grades were suffering. My first question was, "How had it gone from a part-time to a full-time job?" Jayden responded that his Grandmother hadn't been doing well physically and she'd had to quit her part-time job. Jayden had felt obligated to increase his hours at his job and drop a few classes.

I did my best that semester to help Jayden maneuver the path of working and learning, which is often difficult for mature adults to undertake. He passed two classes and failed one, but we talked about focusing our energy on the two classes he'd passed. When the spring semester rolled around, I emailed to ask if he'd selected his classes yet. He responded that he wouldn't be going back to college that spring. His feelings of responsibility for supporting the household far outweighed his desire to go to college.

Jayden's life may not have taken the path that I would have chosen for him. Such a bright, inquisitive mind like his would have flourished in college! I know that the trauma of losing his mother through separation, and subsequently, his Grandmother becoming his whole universe, changed him and molded him into the young man he is today.

It would probably be the "teacher" response to say that I was greatly disappointed by his decision to abandon college after only one semester. However sad I felt that a young man had to make such a difficult decision between supporting his family or going to college, I was proud of his willingness to sacrifice his dreams (if only for now) to help make his Grandmother's life better.

I like to believe that, where there is a desire to help others, there's always great hope for that individual's future.

(A portion of this story originally appeared in Can You See Me published by Belinda Adams in 2018.)

~End of the Day Takeaways~

Meeting Jayden again after 10 years reminded me of all the reasons I'd gone into teaching! His words focused me on touching that one heart, of impacting an individual's life without even knowing you've done it. I'm so thankful for the opportunity to know that I actually accomplished that goal – many times teachers never know of the young lives they have touched!

While we may never know, it may help to remember this young boy whose heart was changed forever. It's difficult for us, as educators, to see possibilities to include fun activities with difficult, fast-paced curriculum and administrators with unrealistic expectations. Yet, two minutes of a fun activity, like Hokey Pokey for a six-year-old made all the difference to Jayden and probably for other students as well.

While there may be those who view Jayden's story as a story of a child who never overcame the trauma of being removed from his dependent mother, I see his story much differently. Jayden could have withdrawn into himself and become a sullen child and student. Jayden could have struck out physically or emotionally towards his grandmother and other adults because of his anger at his situation. He did none of those things.

Instead, he used the situation to push himself to excel in school, and to do his best to make his grandmother proud for the sacrifices she had made to raise him and his younger sister.

I hope someday that Jayden does find his way back to college. Until then, he's still a success in my eyes!

Expressing Compassion and Love

MIKEY: Life's Too Much Work

Mikey was a 7-year-old boy in my 2nd grade class, one year. Sadly, I recall that, each day, he undertook a mission to make himself unlikeable. I've got to give him a great deal of credit because he took on this mission like a dedicated soldier headed into battle!

Regardless of the activity I had planned, he announced, "this is boring" and for every assignment we did, he exclaimed "this is stupid". Notwithstanding his average intelligence, he struggled to learn grade level concepts and lagged behind his peers in academic growth; I think this was mostly due to his unwillingness to engage in any lesson.

Most days, he'd arrive and have a meltdown ore ever making it to his seat. Usually, it was the mere reminder that today was music or asking if he happened to bring his gym shoes for gym. To these innocuous declarations or questions, he'd throw himself on the floor, laying there motionless, and moaning that "school is stupid." Getting him to start the day without some amount of drama was a struggle ... and that struggle continued all day, with all of his teachers, regardless of the subject being studied.

In *Emotion: The On/Off Switch for Learning,* Vail describes why some children may seek this approach to interactions with others. "This is the logical place to make the distinction between rejection – an active, overt reaction - to being neglected or overlooked. While the "invisible child" may be saddened by his or her fate, being unnoticed is far less painful than being pushed away" (Vail, 1994, p. 161). This explains Mikey's actions to make himself as "unlikeable" as possible, thereby assuring it would be his choice, not being ignored or pushed away by his teachers.

common for our kids!

At times, it was excruciating for me to restrain myself from being drawn into a debate by his constant complaining and whining. Even with my best efforts, I'd often find myself exasperated and send him crying to his desk because all my labors at engaging him were not working. He insisted he was right about everything, even when the answer to the math equation was incorrect. He'd refuse assistance and push my hand away as I attempted to show him the mistake in his calculations.

At best, it was a tenuous situation, often made worse by his inconsistent use of his ADHD medication and lack of sleep. Returning from Christmas break seemed to be the height of his discontent in my classroom. One day, I asked him: "Just exactly what is the problem? And what can I do to help you?" To that, with little emotion, he answered, "Nothing. Life is just too much work."

To that answer, I was stunned. I'd never heard such a pronouncement, much less expected to hear something like that from a 7-year-old. As I stood motionless for a moment collecting myself, I saw, perhaps for the first time, the overwhelming sadness on this little boy's face.

I called the social worker to "take him for a walk" to see if she could get him to expand upon his statement and what exactly was making his "life too much work." Not to my surprise, he refused to speak to the social worker, and returned to class to throw himself on the floor beneath his desk, where he laid motionless staring at the ceiling until lunchtime.

That night at home, I determined that even though I couldn't discern the reasons why Mikey was the way he was, I couldn't, with good conscious, allow him to continue to feel dejected and disengaged at school. I decided that, despite his efforts to make himself unlikeable, I was going to "kill him with kindness" so to speak.

The next morning, I greeted him at the bus as always, but this day, I laid on a gigantic smile, informing him emphatically that today was going to be a great day! Not having had too many great days recently, he looked at me very doubtfully, but surprising to say, took my hand as we headed off to the classroom.

When he'd removed his coat, I refused to be drawn into his complaints about why kids couldn't bring toys to school and why school couldn't be fun like video games. Instead, I announced that I needed a "big squeeze" to get the day started as I was feeling a little bit tired. Much to my surprise, he ran over to give me a "big squeeze" around the waist and headed off to his seat.

That day, I made a point to offer him many compliments when I found him doing something he was supposed to be doing. I attempted to field his questions that were unrelated to the topic at hand and managed to get him interested in an activity during reading. He was always talking about being a storm chaser when he grew up, so I'd planned a VENN diagram activity for him to compare a "Hurricane" to a "Tornado". So far, so good, right?

I'd like to tell you that making Mikey feel welcomed, cared for, and accepted in the classroom that day was easy. It wasn't. At the end of the day, I was exhausted! It wasn't easy smiling at a kid who was insisting that his way of doing math (however wrong) was really the right way to do it! It wasn't easy smiling when he stated for the hundredth time that "school was boring" and "why couldn't I be as fun as a video game". But smile I did, and Mikey made it through the day with the fewest meltdowns since returning from Christmas break.

As I put him on the bus for the weekend, I reminded him that Monday was going to be another great day, and I was rewarded with one of his rare smiles and two thumbs up.

That afternoon, as I drove home from school, I reminded myself that I'd better rest up because my campaign to love Mikey, even while he battled, required a great deal of energy, patience, and resistance to his efforts to suck me into his negative perception of school. Thinking back upon the day's events though, I had to smile because it had been a great day for Mikey, and I'd made that happen for him. I hoped he was smiling too as he thought about school and wasn't dreading Monday as much as he normally did!

What I didn't know that day or for a month or so following was that Mikey's home life was nothing like I envisioned. I based my perception on faulty thinking. I mean, he always came to school clean and neatly dressed. Notes sent home for supplies or needing signatures were returned promptly. What I discovered later made me realize the magnitude of my decision to shower Mikey with kindness.

I had known that Mikey's parents had divorced. What I didn't know was that the divorce had been due to Mikey's father's alcohol abuse and his subsequent abuse of Mikey's mother. After a few months of living with Mikey's maternal grandparents, they had moved to an apartment of their own.

Recently, the older sibling had reported to his social worker that Mom had been drinking at home. Dinners had been uncooked, and the younger two children, which included Mikey and his nine-year-old sister, had not been fed and had gone to bed hungry.

Mom was emotionally unavailable for Mikey, and it seemed like the situation was not new. Even though Mikey never mentioned difficulties at home, most likely because he didn't possess the vocabulary or didn't know his homelife wasn't okay. However, his home situation had a major impact on his personality, how he perceived school, and his overall ability to access learning. As a result, his

...iction had been to focus his fears and frustrations

school.

Situations like Mikey's remind me that we, as the teacher, often don't have a clear picture of the lives our students face at home. We can't make assumptions they are receiving the needed attention from their family. I have to remind myself that, whether we know the facts or not, shouldn't keep us from reaching out and engaging all students in whatever way we can, even if it means using all of our personal resolve and patience. Amen! Ll

~End of the Day Takeaways~

Perhaps the biggest detail I had been overlooking when dealing with Mikey was what Vail describes as a child avoiding rejection by pushing away. Or in Mikey's case, making himself unlikeable, which appeared to be his biggest defense in protecting himself from hurt.

RAD - push - pull!

His approach, although probably not a conscious choice on the part of a seven-year-old, had become a habit he'd perfected. When I saw the hurt in his eyes when he talked about his life being too much work, it made me realize that he'd found the only action he knew — avoidance of rejection by not allowing others to get too close to him. RAD

Tobally Calo, kids w/
push/pull

What I learned that day, however, was that he hadn't hesitated one second before running to give me a "big squeeze". This showed me that, despite his tendency to turn away from us, he still longed for love, attention, and acceptance.

Though many of us are aware of the concept Vail talks about that people use to avoid rejection, often we forget or fail to make the connection. "Sometimes it is easy to miss problems. We make unwarranted assumptions of important information. Sometimes we focus so much on school that we miss what's important outside of the school environment" (Kauffman, 2005, p. 40).

Reaching out to him the next day and the day after that was exactly what I planned to do each day, despite his efforts to keep me at arm's length. There were days he responded and worked diligently at his tasks. There were other days when, despite my efforts, he couldn't seem to pull himself together. Regardless, I tried. Even after difficult days, when both of us were exhausted and rumpled, he'd ask for a hug before getting on the bus, then he'd rush to his seat to put his face against the window to wave to me as the bus pulled out. These small actions gave me the resolve I needed to continue to make school a place he didn't dread coming.

Belinda Adams

Building Trusting Relationships

SUNNY: Mom Doesn't Want Me

One year, in my 2nd grade class, I had a student called "Sunny". I say, called Sunny, because that wasn't her real name, but her father had started calling her that as a young toddler and that's the name she went by all of the time.

It didn't take long in my class for me to realize that "Sunny" was a wonderful name for the little girl who arrived each day with smiles. She wanted to be a teacher "just like me" and loved the opportunity to stamp "Homework" or "Good Job" on papers after I had graded them. She was a quick learner, and rushed through her assignments with ease, so she could help me with my work.

One morning, Sunny came to school looking very sad, and I asked if I might have lunch with her that day, to talk about what was bothering her. She had a very sad story to tell.

I knew that Sunny was living with her father and had been since her parents had separated when she was three years old. She had often spoke about her excitement to see her mother, and how much fun she had when she visited her mother at a rural home where she lived with Sunny's grandfather. The previous evening, Sunny's father called her into the kitchen and handed her the phone saying, "Your mom wants to talk to you."

Much to Sunny's confusion, her mom told her that she was moving in with her boyfriend and Sunny would not be coming to visit her. "Forever?" she had asked, and her mom had answered "I'm not sure."

Sunny was devastated by the news, and subsequent feelings of abandonment. "How can she not want to see me, Mrs. Adams?" she'd said through tears during lunch. For that question, I had no answer, and all I could do was squeeze her hand and offer a small smile.

In *When a Hug Won't Heal the Pain*, Monahan writes: "If acknowledging a child's feelings were easy, I'm sure it would be done more frequently. It is, in fact, quite difficult to accept what children say about their feelings. There are so many feelings we wish children would not have" (Monahan, 2005, p. 106).

Sunny took the loss of visitation with her mother very hard. It became difficult to muster a smile, and she rarely wanted to play "teacher" and stamp papers when she completed her work. I spoke with her Dad about the situation and he said he was seeing similar changes at home. Even referring Sunny to meet with the social worker did little to improve the downward spiral of Sunny's previously optimistic outlook on life. I asked if he thought a phone call to Sunny's mom might help, and to that, he shook his head despondently.

In Vail's book, *Emotion: The On/Off Switch for Learning,* she writes, "Rejection hurts. It also moves beyond the social/emotional realm, diminishing academic potential and success" (Vail, 1994, p. 161).

Sunny's sad mood seemed to lift after Christmas break. She'd gotten some wonderful gifts and her father's girlfriend had moved in with her young son. Sunny enjoyed taking care of the little boy and found comfort in having a woman around the house. For these things, I was very grateful.

Sunny never fully returned to her happy-go-lucky self. There always seemed to be a small part of her where she held her sorrow over losing her mother.

Sunny did, however, become a wonderful reader and writer that year in 2nd grade. She loved to write stories about me, going so far as to create a journal called "Mrs. Adams Goes Bananas" and writing story after story about crazy things I might do, and even a few stories about crazy things I DID do!

On Fridays, I'd take the journal home and write back to her. Sometimes, I'd comment on her stories; however, most of the time, I added a paragraph or two about the "Amazing Sunny" who saved the day, usually with true facts like how she always reminded me on days we had library book check-out (or else I'd surely forget).

Woolfolk defines a critical need for all children, and especially those who might be experiencing trauma, and that's the need for "relatedness." She writes, "Relatedness is the need to establish close emotional bonds and attachments with others and reflects the desire to be emotionally connected to the important people in our lives. When teachers and parents are responsive and demonstrate that they care about the children's interests and well-being, the children show high intrinsic motivation" (Woolfolk, 2001, p. 379).

I never lost touch with Sunny during her school years. When she went to middle school, she and her friends would "sneak into" the elementary school on days when middle school started later. And when she went to high school, she'd stop by on days when her classes were over early. I remember laughing about her driving herself over to elementary school, and how old that knowledge made me feel.

She hugged me and said, "You know, I still have that journal of stories I wrote about you! I found it the other day when I was looking for something." I asked what she thought about them now, and she laughed and said, "They're great! I can't believe all of the adventures we dreamed up for the "Bananas Mrs. Adams" and the "Amazing Sunny". I'm going to keep it forever."

Definition of love?
How to spell love?
T-I-M-E!

The ACE's study is valuable for our work. Our families fill this out before enrollment

When Sunny was headed to the 6th grade, I received the following letter.

"Dear Mrs. Adams, Thank you for helping me with reading in 2nd grade. I really appreciate it. Thanks to you I love and enjoy reading! I am so thankful for you are my reading hero! I am at an 8th grade reading level but I wouldn't have been able to be an amazing reader if it weren't for your help.

I will miss seeing you in the halls when I go to middle school. Hey! Did I tell you, I got into honors!

Thanks to you I was able to read and get into honors.

Love, Sunny"

The ACE Study

In Paul Tough's article, *Helping Children Succeed*, he discusses the importance of a study conducted in the 1990's called the Adverse Childhood Experiences (ACE) study. What makes this study so pertinent to this book is the correlation found between childhood trauma and problems in school.

The study considered 10 categories of trauma: 3 categories of abuse, 2 types of neglect, and 5 categories of "seriously dysfunctional households" which included domestic violence, divorced parents, family member incarceration, mental illness and substance abuse problems. Each participant in the study was asked to indicate how many categories he/she had experienced as a child. The following information might surprise you.

Of the children who had experienced 4 or more of the ACE trauma categories, 51 percent had learning or behavior problems in school; striking when compared to the 3 percent of children with an ACE score of zero demonstrating similar school problems.

A second study in 2014 found that that children with two or more experiences of the ACE trauma categories were eight times more likely than children with none to demonstrate behavior problems in school and more than twice as likely to repeat a grade in school. Further, the study concluded that more than half of children have never experienced an adverse event. The other half, the children with at least one ACE indicator, account for 85 percent of the behavior problems that educators see in schools.

Tough, Helping Children Succeed, 2016

Dr. Nadine Burke
Ted talks video

How Some Schools Use This Information

In talking with teachers I have worked with over the years, I learned several of the low-income schools in my district are giving the Adverse Childhood Experiences test to their students. What they are finding is that many of the students score very high on the ACE test, even those in Kindergarten and First Grade!

I was happy to find that under the direction of our superintendent, one school in our district has begun to implement special curriculum that specifically addresses the unique needs of students of trauma. After much research, Kristin Sainsbury, principal, worked with Michael Folta, assistant principal, to obtain a grant for the program. By using the "trauma-informed school" model discussed previously in this book, this school has identified the students with the highest ACE score and provided them with access to differentiated instruction and access to counseling services at the school, while maintaining high academic expectations.

Principal Sainsbury shared some key components of the program which are exactly what students of trauma need. The program identifies students and provides targeted intervention with individualized plans for academic and behavior goals, low student-teacher ratio, with high expectations and accountability. It includes a staff of 5 to provide wraparound mental health services, informed trauma instruction, and ongoing needs assessment.

While too early for hard data, the school has seen an increase in student academic growth, social/emotional awareness, and a decrease in school absenteeism. That's great news for the 100 or so students being provided these services.

However, as statistics in this book show, there are so many more children out there that are suffering from the sometimes-debilitating effects of trauma. Some are able to "hide" it from their peers and teachers; others choose to demonstrate it in defiant ways; yet others are waiting for limited seats in the program, as these types of programs are expensive to implement.

Discussing the program with Principal Sainsbury, she agreed it is a great start for the kids in the program, but she realizes that only a fraction of the students that would benefit from the program are being served. As a result of that knowledge, some of the strategies are being used throughout the school, such as the reworking of the behavior system away from the punitive model to a restorative model that focuses on restoring the student to good standing. Plus restoring anyone or any property the student may have harmed. Building relationships and an awareness of trauma is a focus for all teachers, as is high academic expectations.

The goal of this book is to motivate schools and teachers to focus on the general strategies. If your school doesn't have a trauma program, encourage your administration to look into one. However, whether your school has a similar program or not, it is almost certain that you have students in your room who have experienced trauma that would benefit from the strategies in this book. It is my hope that all teachers can be equipped with the knowledge and strategies they need to recognize the signs of trauma and reach out to students. You have the ability to be a difference for the students in your room and for other students you come in contact with.

I wonder how students of trauma might perform if more schools and teachers were aware of the effects of trauma on children and consciously implemented strategies to help them begin to heal and experience success?

Belinda Adams

TRAUMA & the Older Child

One big difference I noticed when I moved to the 5th grade classroom and dealt with students in that age group was the way in which they responded to trauma in their lives. Very few cried. Very few, at the beginning of the school year (and some never) sought out my assistance or guidance or even just an adult listening ear. Unlike my younger students who seemed to long for an adult to ask, "What's wrong?" these students seemed to send the nonverbal message that they just wanted to be left alone. If I did ask, "What's wrong?" I found I needed to be prepared for a variety of reactions. I experienced everything from comments about ı my own business to no words at all (just a ınd others who shrugged as if to say, "I have what you're talking about!"

The National Child Traumatic Stress Network explains, "Some traumatic experiences occur once in a lifetime, others are chronic or ongoing in a student's life. Many children have experienced multiple traumas, and for too many children, trauma is a chronic part of their lives. Students who have experienced traumatic events may experience problems that impair their day-to-day functioning" (NCTSN, 2008, p. 11).

As a teacher, many times I had to look for clues or I would totally miss the fact that a child's difficulties in school were directly connected to trauma experiences in his or her young life. Students at this age are very adept at hiding trauma in their lives.

We might wonder about why the student's response to my questions varied greatly. We have to remind ourselves that our students, especially those who are older, are seeing the world from two different perspectives. And these contradictory perspectives on life can evoke a variety of strong feelings.

For example, "students are learning from your behavior as they observe how you handle problems in the classroom. They are also learning from the behavior they observe at home. It may be confusing for a student who witnesses domestic violence at home to understand that violence is an inappropriate strategy at school"

(http://www.nctsn.org/trauma-types/early-childhood-trauma).

As educators, we need to be sensitive to the confusion this causes some students. This is not an excuse to accept inappropriate behavior, but an encouragement to find strategies to help students acquire appropriate behaviors as they learn that different settings require different behaviors.

Helping students identify their mixed emotions might be one strategy for helping them to begin to demonstrate appropriate reactions to situations in school, and hopefully, show them that there are alternatives to the behaviors they witness at home (while at the same time making sure our actions and words don't give the impression that we are judging what's happening at home).

It is helpful to explicitly teach students that there are different rules for different situations. School Rules and Home Rules, for example. As I wrote in my previous book, kids understand the need for different rules for different sports. With help, they can also see the need for different rules in different situations.

attunement

It's also helpful for them to see that everyone is constantly facing stressful situations. It might be as simple as "walking" a student through a stressful situation that happened to you at school or at home, telling them how you felt at the moment, your conscious thoughts about your possible reactions and solutions, and consequently, the action that you took. In this way, they begin to see that they are not the only one with stressful situations; they can see others handling stressful situations. *empathy*

In addition, I've found that when students can see me as a "real person," with real personal challenges, both at work and home, they begin to realize that we may not be so different after all. They no longer view me as the adult with all of the answers to life's questions. Instead, they begin to see me as a person who is learning as I go, just as we are expecting them to do. This helps students understand that it is okay to be learning. After all, if Mrs. Adams is still learning and she has already finished college, maybe it is okay if I don't know everything, yet.

I this, again CASA being used.
Less you vs them & more of a connection.

he Day Takeaways~

As part of our schools Positive Behavior Intervention System (PBIS), once a week we teach a lesson on topics such as empathy, perspective, managing emotions, etc. I believe all of these topics are difficult concepts for young minds to embrace, especially those who may come from dysfunctional homes where normalcy is something that occurs in other people's houses, where expressions of such emotions are part of their everyday lives.

Even though we were provided with a "Teaching Manual," there was often a great deal of eye rolling when I played the instructional video of two children using statements like, "What you did really hurt my feelings" or "Can we talk about how that made me feel?" Really? That's not how most children speak to one another under the best of circumstances, and certainly not in a low-income school where students face incredible odds each day.

I'd usually try to "think outside of the box" to design a lesson that would engage them and get them thinking.

One particular lesson was on perspective. I pointed to the definition I'd written on the board reading, "how a person views, or sees things." I explained that for today's lesson we were going to see how things looked from the "perspective" of someone else.

While the students were at lunch, I'd rearranged the furniture, bringing the round table out from near the wall, pushed some desks together, and rolled a free-standing, revolving bookshelf to the center of the room.

I provided each student a blank piece of paper and pencil and stationed them around the room. At first they were confused, then elated that we'd be skipping writing to draw. I positioned students at varying locations, some under the table looking up at the table; some on desks looking at table from above; some on the floor, looking up at the bookshelf, and others sitting on desks looking at the bookshelf.

The assignment was to draw the object from the location they were placed. This direction resulted in peals of laughter and wiggling around, but soon, they settled into the task. Later, they compared the 2 sets of drawings of the table, and likewise, the two sets of drawings of the bookshelf. They were amazed at the difference location could make in how something looked. I smiled and said, "That's seeing something from another person's perspective" and they said, "Really? That's cool!"

Is it really that simple? Can be? If you're willing to think outside the box. I know that being able to share another's perspective is an area where many students of trauma struggle. I like to think that small lessons like this one can help them begin to see another's perspective and learn to better communicate with their peers.

103

Belinda Adams

Fostering Talents

ow Ki do this sometimes or disruptive @ home & not @ school

SHIANA: Couldn't Fall Asleep

One year in my 5th grade class, I had an African American girl who lived with her mother and grandmother in a nearby apartment complex. She had only two modes of operation: charming and compliant or obstinate and disruptive. I would often find myself holding my breath as I waited in the hallway for her to arrive each morning. Generally speaking, the look on her face depicted the kind of day she was going to have.

With students like Shiana, there are many phone calls home, and I got to know the Grandmother very well through our conversations. Sometimes, she'd answer the phone, "What she do now?" For that reason, I tried to make contact with the Grandmother on days when she had a great day rather than always calling about a problem.

I remember only speaking to her Mom once or twice during the first half of the school year. And when I did, she was apologetic, often saying, "Mrs. Adams, I'm doing the best I can." For some reason, I believed her.

As the year progressed, the charming, compliant Shiana pretty much vanished from sight and the obstinate, sullen, disruptive student made a daily arrival. She frequently complained about being tired and not being able to sleep as the cause of her misbehavior. The principal and I decided it was time for a home visit, to see if we could get to the bottom of her issues.

I remember vividly that it was a couple of weeks before Christmas break when we made the home visit. This vision is so vibrant because, the first thing that struck me upon entering the small apartment was the absence of a Christmas tree, wrapped presents, or decorative lights of any kind. There was no sign that Christmas was approaching in this house!

The Grandmother met us at the door and asked us to follow her to where Shiana's mom was resting. Resting? There was a silent hush in the house that can't be described simply as the absence of noise. The blinds were drawn, the lights were turned down, and the principal and I struggled as our eyes adjusted to the darkness.

The Grandmother led us into a bedroom off of the kitchen where I was met with the vision of Shiana's mother, propped up in a wheelchair in a corner of the bedroom. It seemed that every available space in the room was being used. My eyes moved around the room, I guess in a sense, trying to avoid looking at the small form of the woman sitting in a wheelchair. With shame, I realized, I hadn't even known she was sick.

My eyes took in the bed, the bedside table full of medicine bottles, and in what seemed like the only available space, was a hospital monitor and oxygen machine. Finally, my eyes fell on Shiana's mother.

Shiana's mother began talking, and it was such a whisper, I found myself kneeling down in front of her wheelchair, so I could hear her. "I'm so sorry that my girl been causing you problems at school," she said. "I do try my best …", her voice trailed off as she reached for my hand.

I mentioned that Shiana often told us she was tired and couldn't sleep. At that comment, Shiana's mother turned tearful eyes towards mine. "I guess, that's my fault. You see, she sleeps in here with me …" She hesitated as my eyes again swept the bedroom, for the first time, seeing this room from Shiana's point of view.

I waited, and she continued, "I can't help crying most of the night. It's the pain, you know? I try to not let her hear me crying, but sometimes, it just hurts so much…"

I swallowed back a lump in my throat that seemed to be the size of a golf ball and found myself clinging tightly to her hand. I forgot most of the rest of the conversation I'd intended to have with Mom, and instead, told her we would continue to work with her daughter at school. What else was there to say?

As the Grandmother walked us to the door, I asked about her daughter's prognosis, and she quietly shook her head from side to side. "She don't have long," was all she said. Silently, the principal

and I walked back to the car and drove b[ ]
school without a word passing between us.

I'd like to say that Shiana's mother m
miraculous recovery and that Shiana finished out
her 5th grade year as a stellar student. To both, I
must answer no. Shiana continued to be
noncompliant and uncooperative and tired for the
rest of the school year.

In her book, *Children and Trauma,* Monahan
describes what we were witnessing in our
classroom: "Remembering and mourning involve
great inner and external struggle for many children.
The wish to forget and avoid continuously clashes
with the child's unwanted recall of memories and
feelings. ...There is inevitable pain, anger, and loss
for children during this phase. The inner turbulence
is most often evident in the disturbed and disturbing
behavior that signals distress, in their nightmares,
reenactments, and raging determination to seize
control of every situation" (Monahan, 1995, p. 125).

It was that need to control everything that
seemed to be the most difficult for us to deal with in
the classroom. And yet, it seemed, unavoidable,
given her home situation and her state of mind. The
district's behavior specialist had explained to us,

This is so true!

that often students in this type of situation struggle with guilt. When they are having a good day, they remember the parent struggling. Often, out of guilt, they engage in behaviors to turn things around so that the day changes from good to bad.

My partner teacher and I were able to see glimpses of the 5th grade girl she wished she could be when we bought her a new "pleather" coat she had been admiring on another girl in the class next door. She wore that coat every day, even when the weather was hot. At other times, we'd compliment it, she'd smile just for a moment, and say, "I know. Isn't it great?"

She'd forget her troubles for moments of time, for example, when she tried out for the School Talent Show. We let her practice for the talent show in our classroom day after day during lunch because she wasn't able to stay for the formal practices after school as she didn't have a ride home. She loved that talent show. She really shined as she bopped to the hip-hop song she'd chosen. She'd only been able to participate that night because I'd promised her that I'd drive her home afterward.

Too soon, that evening after all of the children had congratulated one another, it was time for my husband and I to drive her home. From the front seat, I watched as the shadow of sadness settled on her face once again.

When the summer arrived, we heard from others that she, her mother, and her Grandmother had moved to the city to live with Shiana's aunt. Shortly after their move, Shiana's mother passed away. That's the last I ever heard.

One of the most difficult issues with working with many children of trauma is the high rate of transience, especially for students suffering from neglect, abuse, or poverty. As a teacher, I have to remind myself to focus on the gains I have made with each student for that year. For Shiana, I concentrated on the joy she found in wearing her new jacket and performing in the talent show. As a teacher, you may be disappointed, but many times all we are able to do is plant a few seeds of hope and joy, giving someone else the opportunity to water and nurture success. I pray that, in Shiana's new school, she has found another teacher who will see the hurting little girl behind the fierce façade and find a way to make her smile as she learns positive ways to deal with the trauma in her life.

~End of the Day Takeaways~

Although there was no action my partner teacher and I could take that would change the fact that Shiana's mother was dying of cancer, we could attempt to create moments of her day when she could forget that tragic fact. Discovering her love for dancing and her desire to participate in the Annual School Talent Show was an accident. However, we capitalized on that love, and gave her opportunities within our classroom to foster that love. In one small way, we allowed her a few moments to be a 10-year-old girl with aspirations of being a dancer and forget about her sad reality at home.

I'd like to think that we made a positive impact on Shiana, despite her efforts to keep a distance between us. Secretly, I hope she's still wearing her jacket with a smile!

In Vail's book, she states the difference between being able to deal with trauma and not being able to deal with trauma comes down to a few factors, including "One teacher who takes a personal interest in the child, or acts as a role model, counselor, or confidante, can be a powerful force for resilience" (Vail, 1994, p. 39). Sometimes, showing personal interest is all we can do. The littlest things often give children enough hope, so they can withstand the pain and possibly make a difference in their perspective on life.

Seeing the Child, Not the Trauma

JAMES: Living His Best Life Each Day

Having a student in your classroom with a tumor in his brain is pretty rare. However, I had a student named James in my 5th grade, special education classroom who had just that!

Just a few weeks into the school year, it was apparent that James was a very smart young man. What was most memorable about him was his sense of calm and his quiet, respectful manner. He was always the most pleasant, helpful, and kind student. He was the first to offer assistance, and he's the only student I've ever had who held doors open for teachers.

I was aware that James had a cancer diagnosis and that he'd undergone several surgeries before coming to my 5th grade class. What I didn't know, when I met James, was that he also had an inoperable brain tumor. His mother told me about it when she came for curriculum night. Quietly, she explained that he was given 6 months to live … one and a half years previously. Amazing, I thought!

Mom told me that James went for a brain scan every two months as the doctors were watching the size of the tumor. For the past year and a half, it hadn't grown at all, much to the surprise of his doctors and relief of his family and friends.

When I met James, I wasn't aware of the statistics about childhood cancer. I learned later through personal research that over 11,000 children are diagnosed with new cancers each year and that 250,000 children are cancer survivors in the United States (CPTS, Medical Events, 2008, p. 2).

Knowing this information and James' diagnosis caused me to view James from a different perspective. Instead of appearing to be a young man living on borrowed time, James was a young man committed to living the best life he could each day.

One day, while he and I were waiting for the rest of the class to return from a bathroom break, James quietly asked, "My mom told you about my condition, didn't she?" I answered, "Yes." He seemed to contemplate that for a minute before he simply said, "Thanks." Our conversation was stopped by the arrival of the rest of the class, so I didn't have the opportunity to ask what it was he was thanking me for.

As the months of that school year flew by, I found myself becoming extremely attached to James. It wasn't the knowledge of the tumor that made him special; it was *who* he was! Unlike other children who might be facing death, he never said, "Why should I learn this stuff?" or "Who cares about that because I might not even be alive?"

Nope, that would have been completely out of character for James. He showed interest in learning new things and supported my efforts in getting other students interested as well. He asked a lot of questions and never seemed to get tired of my stories. For James, each day held a new opportunity.

Further, James pushed me as an educator to hold him accountable for learning the standards just like everyone else, even when I knew he'd been at the hospital the previous day for his brain scan. When I didn't ask, "Where's your homework?" he'd say, "Here's my homework. I did it at the hospital yesterday."

One day, after school as I sat grading papers, he came back to school because he'd forgotten his homework and his father had brought him back to get it. He ran down to the class while dad waited in the car. I helped him retrieve his homework from his desk and walked with him back down the hallway.

While it had been months since he'd said "Thanks," I hadn't forgotten, and for the life of me, I hadn't been able figure out what he was thanking me for. I turned to him as he headed for the doors and said, "James, that day you said 'thanks,' do you remember that?" He smiled, "Sure I do." I said, "Well, I hope this doesn't sound ridiculous, but can I ask you what you were thanking me for?"

James stopped with his hand on the door and said in his quiet manner, "I was thanking you for never making me feel different than the other kids. I was thanking you for not feeling sorry for me. I was thanking you for being my teacher." "Oh," I answered, and then said, "It's my pleasure to do it!" He smiled that knowing smile I'd come to recognize so well and said, "I know. See you tomorrow, Mrs. Adams."

James' tumor didn't grow that year in the 5th grade or next year in the 6th grade. He'd stop by my classroom occasionally to see how I was (yes, the one with the brain tumor was checking on me!). He talked about his dreams to go out for the football team in high school. "That is, if my Mom lets me. She always worries about me."

James' family moved out of state after he finished the 6th grade. I never knew how James' health situation turned out. I guess, there's a part of me that's grateful for that. As my husband had pointed out, he was fairly certain I'd need *counseling if that boy had passed away. In my mind, I imagine James as he would be now in his Senior year of high school. I like to think he got to play football.*

When I think about that year with James, I realize he reminded me of the fact that most kids just want to be treated like "kids," regardless of their individual circumstances. His words of "Thanks" kept me mindful that it's so easy to touch a young heart … sometimes just by following your own!

Thinking back about James and his terminal condition, I often wondered how he handled the situation as well as he did. Yes, part of how he handled it was merely his calm nature and caring heart. However, I also thought about the support he received from home, his mother, father and brother. I recalled that Mom never asked for special consideration for her son because of his condition. She hadn't expected anything more than for me to be his teacher. Most of us would agree that family support can make all the difference in the life of a child, and even more so, when the child is facing such an uncertain future.

A study conducted by Center for Pediatric Traumatic Stress supports that notion: "Parents are key resources for their child's emotional recovery after a traumatic injury" (CPTS, Medical Events, 2008, p. 52).

※ this is true for a woman's recovery + response to being raped + how her mother supports her.

"Children need to be reminded of their strengths and their competence. They like to hear about difficulties they have overcome in the past. ...

Parents who focus on the image of their child as a strong survivor can hold this image up for the child through remembering and retelling stories about the child's competence. ...

Children welcome the images of their strengths and resilience that parents offer."

(Monahon, 1995, p. 123-124).

As teachers, we can do the same. Remind students how much they have learned, or how much they have matured in a behavioral or emotional aspect. It's important to remind the student of successes.

~End of the Day Takeaways~

Over the course of many years of teaching at-risk youth (many of whom had suffered some form of trauma), I was asked, "How do you get your students to tell you so much about themselves?" It seems that other teachers who had the same students, would hear from me that the student's parents were facing a divorce, or a father had been sent to jail, for example. I didn't really have an answer at the time, and I just shrugged.

As I reflected on that question, I wondered how it was that students confided in me because I don't consider myself a nosy, over-inquisitive teacher. And for anyone who has worked with children of trauma, asking too many questions usually results in the student shutting down completely. Then one day, the answer occurred to me. *Just listen*

Ever since my early days of teaching, I've always had what teachers refer to as a "bean table" or round table where students would gather in small groups to work with me. It's usually part of student rotations, where students make their way from independent work, or reading, to computer stations and to my table. It's always their favorite "rotation" as they come to enjoy that one-to-four teacher attention.

As students work at that table with their group, it often becomes more like a dinner table. Trust is built between the student, the teacher, and their peers. Students begin to share about their personal lives. I believe that teachers who listen develop rapport that helps failing students want to succeed and students who feel hopeless about their life begin to look for hope.

Not all issues are resolved at that table; however, it certainly opens the door for them to feel "safe" in sharing. Many times, I've asked confidentially, if we might include the social worker in a subsequent conversation. Or asked, later, how I might be able to help them with their situation.

Sadly, knowledge doesn't change their situation, but often, sharing with an adult helps them feel they are no longer alone or isolated in their situation.

I always try to let my students know that, "the way things are right now," doesn't have to be "the way things stay". They have a chance to change things for themselves for the future. *Love this.*

Belinda Adams

Showing Diligence & Family Support

* keep showing up over + over again.

DeSHAUN & BRIAN: Men of the House

One year, I had 2 brothers in my 5th grade special education classroom, although they were not twins. DeShaun was in the 5th grade because he had failed the 3rd grade and Brian was in the 5th grade because he was a 5th grader. Fortunately, I taught reading and writing in both the morning and afternoon and that gave me the flexibility to place one student in my AM class and the other in my PM class because two brothers couldn't have been more different than these two!

DeShaun was a "quiet giant" of a young man as he became known to my partner teacher and me. He was larger than his 5th grade peers, very shy, and introverted. He rarely participated in classroom discussions and avoided being called to the smartboard to answer questions. He liked sitting in the back of the room and seemed to do his best not to get noticed. I recall, a few weeks into the school year that one of the other students angled his head towards DeShaun and asked, "Is that dude all right? I mean, he never ever says nothing!" I responded that, "Yes, DeShaun is fine. He just chooses to be a great thinker instead of talking." I could see by the shy smile on his face that DeShaun liked that answer.

Conversely, Brian who is in my afternoon class was a very boisterous, busy boy. He found reasons (many of them) to be out of his seat, wandering around the room. He enjoyed doing mischievous things, such as taking someone's pencil while he walked back and waiting with a smile for them to notice. To these events and more, he always claimed complete innocence!

There was one thing both boys did have in common, and that was neither of them liked to do any class work, regardless of the subject being taught. DeShaun showed his reluctance by sitting quietly and doing nothing but doodling in the corners of his papers, hoping that he'd be so quiet we'd forget to ask him how he was doing. Brian, on the other hand, found many excuses for not working, like stating, "I don't have a pencil" or "This is too hard" or "Can I go to the bathroom?" Let the list go on. Regardless of how they chose to express it, neither of them seemed to accomplish very much during the school day! So true!

That's how I met their mother. I called her in for a conference to talk about the boys' reluctance to do any class work and to see if she might have any suggestions for encouraging them. I was not prepared to meet the woman I met.

One afternoon shortly after, I was called down to the office by the secretary announcing that the boys' mother had arrived and been placed in the conference room. When I got there, I'm pretty sure I stood there motionless in the doorway for what seemed like 2 minutes (although I'm sure it was only 20 seconds or so). Mom looked very young, and I mean, very young! How could she possibly be the mother of a boy who was 11 and a boy who was 10. Further, she had 2 other children with her, a toddler who looked to be about 2 years old and an infant in a car seat. Wow, I was floored!

During our conference, Mom explained that the family had been forced to move several times as they were trying to get away from the abusive father of the children. Mom said that she was not happy with their current living situation in the low-income housing development, but it was either that or the car. All through our conversation, the toddler seemed to be everywhere in that conference room, all at once! She took books off the bookshelf, emptied the pencils from the holder and scattered paper clips all across the room. Mom tried several times to get her to stop, but it soon became apparent that Mom had very little control over the busy toddler and was further distracted by the constant crying and whining coming from the infant in the car seat. What a scene!

No wonder she was forthcoming in telling me she had very little control over getting the boys to complete their work at home or school, and that they had been that way in school for as long as she could recall. I left that meeting feeling very overwhelmed ... for her! Later, I found out through the social worker that Mom was only 27 years old, living on her own with four children, an abusive significant other looking for her, and barely making ends meet.

Mom became a frequent visitor at our school that year, especially the first few months when it seemed that Brian found many new and frustrating ways to break the classroom and school expectations and required a consequence. To all of these meetings, Mom appeared with the younger children, looking disheveled and overwhelmed with the situation.

Around Thanksgiving, Mom contacted our school social worker who had met with her several times and saw both the boys for weekly social work sessions. Mom was reaching out to ask for assistance in getting food for a Thanksgiving meal. She said she had not been able to find any work nor suitable daycare for the younger ones that made it financially worthwhile for her to go to work. Working with our outside agencies, the social worker and I were able to get enough donations so that the family could enjoy a Thanksgiving meal, including a turkey (something none of the children had had before, I later learned).

Mom reached out to us many times during that school year, asking for financial assistance when the boys needed money to go on field trips and buying Christmas gifts, etc. We did the best we could to find resources for the Mom and directed her to the local food pantry as well.

If you're wondering how the boys were progressing during all of this, I'll answer honestly and say, they were not progressing at all. DeShaun had shown little academic improvement. It was near impossible to assess Brian, as he refused to take any assessments seriously, casually checking boxes and circling things and quickly turning in his papers with little regard for whether or not they were the right answers.

When that school year was over, I'll be honest and say that I breathed a sigh of relief they'd be moving on to the 6th grade and sent a quick, silent prayer upwards for the 6th grade teachers. When I inquired the following year, I learned that they hadn't changed their ways. Kauffman explains the lasting effects of these boys' trauma by saying that, "When the child's primary healing environment, the family, is massively disrupted emotionally or physically, recovery can be complicated by loss and chaos" (1998, p. 62).

Fast forward three years to when the boys were high school freshman. The year I had DeShaun and Brian, I had a paraprofessional (teacher's aide) who was working with me while she completed her master's degree in teaching. She was now a math teacher at the high school. Both of us were surprised when she texted me on the first day of school to report that Brian was in her 1st period math class!

I didn't hear much from her about the boys, as she didn't have DeShaun in class but saw him infrequently in the hallway, and she said that "Brian was up to the same old tricks". Sigh. After a few months, I became engrossed in my own challenges as it seems my current class generally absorbs most of my attention.

Early in the spring, I received a text from my friend at the high school with a photo of a math test with a 94% written at the top but the name was hidden by a post-it. She asked if I could guess who had gotten an "A" on the final exam, and I couldn't fathom an answer. In my defense, she did have several of our students that year, and one girl we'd had 4 years previously had been doing very well in her class. I answered that I didn't have a clue. The next text took me by surprise. She had removed the post-it and the name at the top was "Brian". "Our Brian?" I asked excitedly. "Yes!", she answered. Both of us were elated that he had done so well.

I guess the big idea of this story is: we never know how much of what we are teaching is being "soaked up" by our students. Even those who seem to make it their mission to act as though they are learning as little as possible. Brian was learning math all along, gaining those basic skills, or he wouldn't have had the skills to do the higher-level math in high school. It's easy to make assumptions about students, especially when their efforts to fight the learning process are as obvious as Brian's had been that year. However, it hadn't stopped me and my partner teacher from keeping our expectations high and holding him accountable for the work, even if it meant staying in for recess or missing a preferred activity.

Nope, we were not his favorite teachers; however, I'd like to think that as he grew up and matured, he had to give us a little credit for giving him the foundational skills to help him be successful in high school. Even if he didn't consciously, we know we did our best!

We knew the obstacles in his life that were causing some of his acting out behaviors in school, namely the domestic violence upon his mother that he had witnessed, and further complicated by frequent moves and lack of personal and financial resources at home. Again, we didn't let that knowledge become a reason for us to excuse his behavior or allow our sympathy to keep us from holding him accountable for learning.

That's not to say that we didn't go out of our way to make sure Mom had the resources she needed so they had Thanksgiving dinner and presents at Christmas. At times, when we hadn't been able to locate outside agencies, we were willing to open our own wallets, if necessary, to give them the necessities we felt all children are entitled to.

~End of the Day Takeaways~

One summer, after a particularly challenging school year, I retrieved all of the books about teaching students who learn outside the box from my bookshelf. I read them and contemplated what the authors had to say. Most importantly, I had to visualize, as we all do, what those strategies looked like in my classroom. Because how they look in my classroom might not "fit" another teacher's teaching style or classroom management.

I decided my classroom needed to be filled with a sense of hope; hope that this year, each student could be successful! I made posters with mottos saying, *"If you don't know the answer, we'll figure it out together"* and *"It's only failure if you give up."* I made them myself because I wanted the students to notice, right away, that they were different than the store-bought posters, hopefully demonstrating immediately that they were important to me! Because I've learned that if it's important to the teacher, it becomes important to the students that respect you as well!

As a 5th grade teacher, I taught a morning and an afternoon block of reading and writing. I flipped my class with my partner teacher while she taught math, social studies, and science.

As the classes got settled those first few days of school, we had the usual talk about classroom expectations and consequences. However, I told them that, this year, it was going to be entirely different than any classes before them. Right away, I saw I had their interest. I explained that each class would select a "theme song" that would represent the kind of class they wanted to be. (Of course, I'd already narrowed down their choices. With some carefully guided questions, they soon had my selections on the board and voted as a class for the winning song.)

One class chose my favorite inspirational song by Michael Jackson, *The Man in the Mirror*, and the other class chose a Bruno Mars song, *Count on Me*. I printed out the song lyrics and we spent some time discussing what the words meant and how the students could use those words to guide their actions. It was surprising to hear some of the insightful ideas they came up with for using the lyrics to represent themselves.

I'm fairly certain my partner teacher wanted to burn me at the stake by the end of school, but fortunately, she didn't. Because, we began each class period with a sing-along to the song and video. Some of the kids even came up with a group dance for their class song.

It's interesting as I look back on that school year. I haven't used this strategy every year, and I wonder, did I need a little hope, too?

Belinda Adams

Opening Up Your Heart

DAVID: Life Changed in a Split Second

One year, I had a 5th grade student in my special education, self-contained class who challenged me from the moment he arrived. It seemed he wanted to assure himself, the class, and me that this year was going to be like all of the previous years, and he was going to spend most of it in detention, doodling, and wasting the school hours away.

Sadly, for him, he hadn't met any teachers with the determination of my partner teacher and me. We'd seen many "David's" come and go over the years. We were ready for him, ignoring behaviors that didn't disrupt learning and finding outrageous reasons to compliment him, anything from "great haircut" to "I love the way you included these drawings at the bottom of your writing because the visual really adds to the story you created."

Much to David's bewilderment, he started to participate more in class, sat up most of the time, and did his best to avoid detention. I always think he was afraid he'd miss some ridiculous ploy on the part of his teachers to engage everyone! When he saw me years later at middle school, he'd said, "Remember that time, you and Mrs. Pirog had us doing math to music? Our music?! Rap! And not the kind of sappy stuff you listen to. It was great!"

David began to make academic progress as well, finding it much more entertaining to stay in class and read books, be on the computer, and spend time with his friends. My partner teacher and I were elated. Then an incident occurred in the early spring that changed the trajectory of David's life!

Unbeknownst to his teachers, it was well known to everyone else that David's family, including his older brother and his mother, were part of a gang. Unfortunately for David and his family, it was a rival gang of the one that was predominant in the housing complex where they lived. These facts resulted in much conflict between David's family and the members of the rival gang, their neighbors.

We heard from the principal that, one afternoon, David's mom was riding in a vehicle with David's Aunt when, the Aunt veered the vehicle onto the sidewalk and headed straight for three high school students who had been making trouble for the family. The Aunt drove the vehicle to the point of blocking one of the boys between her vehicle, the wall of the apartment and another vehicle. The boy was able to escape, and the Aunt and Mother disappeared before the police arrived. However, after reviewing camera footage, both the Aunt and David's mother were arrested. Needless to say, David was devastated at the loss of his mother and backlash of neighbors and friends.

However, what neither of us expected was the anger David felt – towards everyone, it seemed. Overnight, he became sullen,  disengaged from the class and the teachers, and found ways to ditch school whenever possible.

I recall one day keeping David in from recess, and saying quietly, "David, I am so scared I am losing you. Day after day, you drift further away is class, your friends, and me. You have

o far this year, and I want to see you

to learn." When he didn't respond, I said on the verge of tears, "Can't you see you're breaking my heart, David?"

Hearing the crack in my voice, he finally looked up and said, "I know you care, but there ain't nothing you can do that can change things! I've got to protect my family! And school is for babies," he finished defiantly and asked if he could leave for lunch. What else could I possibly add to what he'd already said? Not a thing.

We didn't give up on David that year. We continued in our efforts to engage him; however, it was clear that the "David" who thought he could be a better student had been replaced by a "David" who was more interested in "making someone pay" for his situation in life. Vail provides additional insight into David's mindset: When a child feels "estranged from the adult world, he brings with him into the classroom emotional habits of mistrust, confusion, defensiveness, and resentment" (Vail, 1994, p. 225).

Too often, it's easy for us to tell ourselves that situations like David's exist somewhere else, like some downtown housing complex with bars on the windows. However, that is not always the case. According to Children and Trauma, Kauffman states that "When the violence results in death of a parent, disruption of home and caretaking, or involvement in interminable criminal proceedings, the child faces the multiple stresses of dealing with loss, trauma, and family disorganization" (1998, p. 14)

When our students are faced with situations as unpredictable and devastating as this one, it is sometimes the teacher that must offer the stability and affirmations when the family resources are not there to provide them.

I met David again when he was 15-years-old. Due to his lack of interest in school, he was 15 and in the 8th grade! He hadn't been allowed to go to the next grade, and being the tallest kid in middle school, didn't seem to faze him a bit. I asked if he remembered me, and he patted me on the shoulder, and said, "Of course, I do. You're the one that thought you could stop the gang," and walked on with his friends.

I'd like to believe that stories like David's are rare, but statistics can't hide the fact. A 2009 Department of Justice survey showed that 60% of children had been exposed to violence in the past year (justice.gov).

It's difficult for me to process or understand, especially when I recall my own middle-class upbringing. However, these traumatic events occur in the lives of our students, whether gang violence, death of a parent, domestic abuse, or parental incarceration. Knowing this, and the possible trauma that violence may cause, we have to do our best to help them deal with their hurt and anger.

I'll admit that it isn't easy as an educator to concede that not every child we try to help will be successful in getting past trauma in their lives to learn. Even as I write this, I wonder where is David today? Does he recall that someone cared enough about him to tell him? I hope he does!

"A complaint I have often heard through the years from challenging students is that they are never understood" (Benson, 2014, p. 31).

While David struggles to find his way and I strive to accept that I can't change his life situation, I can only be thankful for the time in my classroom

that I had with him to provide the opportunity for him to feel like a success in school and to relate to his teachers and peers (probably for the first time in his academic life). I can't focus on where his life is headed or where he will end up because no one knows the answer to that.

* Great insight on knowing you can't be attached to the outcomes.

Belinda Adams

Accepting What You Cannot Change

DAVION: Nine Too Many

One year, I had a lanky, African American boy named Davion in my 5th grade, special education classroom. He appeared to move like a giraffe, seemingly all arms and legs. He was a charmer, too, often working an extra 5 minutes of recess out of me with a flash of his charismatic smile!

The issue with Davion was that he seemed to always be sleepy. He had a very difficult time making it through independent reading because, even if it was a book he liked, sitting stationary for longer than 10 minutes would cause him to fall asleep. It seemed as the day progressed, it became more and more difficult for him to keep his eyes open and concentrating on any kind of curriculum was generally out of the question.

My partner teacher and I tried to speak with him about getting to bed earlier each evening, and each time, he'd mutter something about "trying to do better" and look away. Attempts to call home to speak to his parents about the issue were futile because they had no working phone in the home. Notes were sent home, but it seemed that support from home was not going to happen.

Even though my partner teacher and I felt sad about how tired he seemed to be, we had expectations for all of the students in our classroom and allowing them to sleep 80% of the day wasn't one of them.

This resulted in Davion frequently being held in from lunch recess to work with us one one-on-one to help him get his classwork done. Some days, this approach was met with cooperation, but there were other days, he'd become very angry with us for keeping him in.

One day, after he'd stormed out of class, I asked him to sit with me on the steps in the stairwell, so we could talk. I began to ask questions about his home life.

I had known he had a large family, but I was surprised to learn from Davion that day that he was the oldest of nine children. The oldest was Davion, age 10, and the youngest was a newborn that had arrived a month earlier. "Wow!" I told him. "What's that like? Having so many kids in one house?" "Crazy" was the word that came to his lips immediately. Yes, I bet, I thought to myself.

I asked why it was that he was so tired every day, even though I had a pretty good idea with that many kids in one apartment. Davion looked up from his scuffed shoes and said, "It's all because of Davey." "Really? Who's Davey?" I asked. Davion went on to explain that each of the older children (Davion, age 10, Darla, age 9, and Dana, age 8) were each assigned a toddler to look after when they got home from school each day. When I asked "Why?" he looked at me as if I was the slowest person on the planet. "Because my mom is tired after doing that all day while we're at school, that's why." "Oh" was all I could think to say.

Davion went on to tell me that little Davey was his responsibility after school, and Davey was not good at going to bed at night. Davion said that when it was bedtime, all Davey wanted to do was play and run around the house. Davion had strict instructions from his mother not to go to sleep before Davey and not to wake her if she was sleeping.

"So, that's why I'm so tired, Mrs. Adams," he replied. "And I'm sure there's nothing I can do about it 'til Davey starts listening to me!" I gave Davion a small side hug and thanked him for sharing this information with me. I promised I'd keep it in mind if he promised to do his best with his work when he was awake.

I'd like to say that things improved for Davion that year, but they didn't. The situation pretty much stayed the same, with Davion being more awake on some days, and falling asleep on others. I'd also like to say that Davion made a lot of progress that year academically, but even though he made some progress he trailed behind his peers in growth, despite trying to help him learn one-on-one.

Even though he never caught up on his sleep or became the top reader in the class, I think he found a place in our classrooms where he could find reprieve, forget about his babysitting responsibilities, and for a little while each day, just be a 10-year-old boy in the 5th grade! Sometimes, things are out of our control and the most we can do is provide a small refuge for a student.

What Davion was experiencing is termed by some experts as parentification, or in other words, when a child has to take on a role of a parent in one way or another. In Davion's case, it was "instrumental parentification" where he was expected to take on the responsibilities of caring for a younger sibling. This parentification results when a child's responsibilities surpass ordinary expectations for an older child to help out occasionally with small household tasks". According to David Hosier, author of Childhood Trauma: Emotional Abuse, expecting too much from a child in this way puts them in a position to grow up too fast, essentially stealing the child's youth (Hosier, 2015).

At the end of that school year, Davion announced they were moving to another apartment in another town. I never knew how things were for Davion in the future. I can only hope that as little Davey grew older, less "parenting" would be required of Davion, and he would have a teacher that could help him make up for lost time, both as a child and a student.

Before the end of the school year, I received a candy bar with a note attached from Davion's mother. It read:

"Thanks for being a great teacher to Davion. He never had one before. Thanks for taking your time with him and his work. I know he can be difficult at times, but I do appreciate all that you do."

Signed, Davion's Mom

~End of the Day Takeaways~

As I think about Davion today, I think of the assumptions I've made along the way that has led my thinking astray. Too often, when we see a child who is not getting enough sleep, our first thought is this child is not receiving the parental attention they need or that parents just don't care.

That's a conjecture I've learned to try to avoid. In Davion's case, his mom was doing the best that she could, given the family situation. If I want to reach that student, I've got to put aside my own thoughts about parents having so many children they can't give each the proper attention. After all, my opinion is irrelevant to the child's situation, and opinions rarely result in actions of compassion and empathy. I have to deal with the current reality, not complain about what should have been.

I don't question that Davion's mother loved her children and wanted them to do well in school. Her lack of resources to be emotionally and physically available for Davion at this time was beyond my control. Helping Davion feel safe to express his situation and frustrations was probably the best gift I could provide.

Belinda Adams

Keeping Expectations High

SHANIQUA: When Pain Steals Motivation

I've had a great deal of interesting things occur on "supply drop-off" night. I've had parents warn me of their child's behavior, I've had children show up with no supplies (just a smile and curiosity over their new teacher), and excitement when a student arrives with an older sibling only for us to realize I'd been the older sibling's teacher as well!

Most students are slightly shy, but gladly take my hand when I put it out to introduce myself. They seem happy to "choose" where they would like to sit the first day, and always take a few moments to casually walk around the room to "check things out".

As parents and children leave, they seem relieved to know I don't have horns or a broomstick and that our classroom looks very welcoming.

However, one year, I had a 5th grade student named, Shaniqua. She didn't fit into any of the descriptions above. Instead, when introductions were being made, this young girl was openly crying. Not a reaction I'd experienced thus far in my teaching career, not even with first grade students.

I distracted her with taking her supplies and having her select a desk of her choice while I took the opportunity to speak privately with her father. He quickly explained that his wife, and Shaniqua's mother, had passed away while she was in 3rd grade, and coming to a new school for 5th grade appeared to be a change she felt she couldn't face. I thanked him for his honesty, expressed my sympathy, and promised she'd be in good hands with my colleague and me. As she left, I gave her a little side hug and assured her that we'd get through 5th grade together. She looked doubtful to say the least.

Much to my surprise, Shaniqua quickly adjusted to the classroom routines, and seemed to

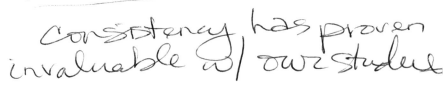

consistency has proven invaluable w/ our student

find comfort in a predictable schedule and structure. Another surprise: It didn't take long for my colleague and me to realize that Shaniqua was a very bright girl. She was smart, quick to complete her classwork, and the first to raise her hand during class discussions. It was very clear that this young lady did NOT belong in a special education classroom!

After speaking with the social worker at her previous elementary school, I learned that there had been some significant behavior and emotional changes in Shaniqua following her mother's sudden death. Her teacher explained that, following the death of her mother in 3rd grade, Shaniqua had missed quite a bit of school. When she did come to school, she was withdrawn and participated little in classroom discussions or classwork. When her reading and math levels showed no improvement at the beginning of 4th grade, her team made a decision to place her in special education classes. There, they reasoned, she could get more individualized attention in a smaller class environment. While this may have seemed like a good plan at the time, I thought the situation needed another approach.

My colleague and I met with her to tell her we'd noticed how smart she was. We were awarded with a smile, saying "I'm glad you noticed!" I prefaced the following conversation by validating the trauma she had experienced. I explained that I couldn't even begin to imagine the pain she must have felt at the passing of her mother, and I was sure she continued to feel that pain and miss her mother every day.

I expounded by telling her that, while we both understood the trauma she had experienced over the loss of her mother, we weren't going to let that effect our expectations of her work. I told her my goal was for her to be back in the general education classroom by the following year. Reluctantly, she looked at us as if to say, "Well, good luck with that!"

Throughout the year, there were many tears of frustration on her part when she just didn't "feel" like working; however, my colleague and I kept our expectations high for her. I'd find myself wanting to comfort her, but instead, pushed the Kleenex box closer to her and continued on. I pushed her, prodded her, and, sometimes, held her in from lunch to complete the work I knew she was very capable of doing.

Together, we made it through the school year and she progressed more than two grade levels in both reading and math. She was off to the general education classroom for 6th grade! Further, we'd helped her learn a valuable lesson in that she could still mourn the passing of her mother while continuing to grow her reading, writing, and math skills. I think she realized that she had a great deal more motivation than she'd dared to dream about.

About the second week of school the following year, Shaniqua appeared at my door during my lunch time with a couple of her friends to tell me that she'd been accepted to be part of a fund-raising group in the 6th grade that took a leadership role in the school. I congratulated her and asked her to introduce me to her friends. She pointed to each, providing their name, and when it came time to introduce me, she said with a smile, "This is the teacher who kicked my butt every day last year!" We hugged, and I told her it was only done out of my faith in her abilities. She laughed and said, "I'll never forget it, and I know where to go if I need my butt kicked if I'm slacking off." I assured her I didn't think that was going to happen.

(A portion of this story appeared in Can You See Me, 2018.)

Dad wrote:

"Mrs. Adams, Thank you for giving my girl hope to continue with school and also believe in herself. You brought out the best in her!
> *Thank you,*
> *Shaniqua's dad".*

~End of the Day Takeaways~

While Shaniqua's situation was different than most others I had encountered in my classroom, it was easy to see that, deep down, she wanted others to see how bright she was! She longed to share the knowledge she knew, despite the trauma of missing her mom. Because we didn't let our sympathy cloud our judgement, her teachers were able to open doors for her that previously had been closed. My partner teacher and I gave her the opportunity to shine!

"Motivation starts with an idea and a hope, gathers momentum, and sustains a plan" (Vail, 1994, p. 7).

In Shaniqua's case, it was hope for her future, that somehow, it could be better than she had ever imagined!

Belinda Adams

Giving Students a Voice

JEFFREY: No Home of His Own

Even working in a low-income school, it's fairly uncommon to have a student be declared "homeless." Most of my students either rented an apartment or lived with family members. However, over the course of my teaching career, a few students have been "declared" homeless by the school district, meaning the family had no residence of their own. For example, one family was living in a homeless shelter where they occupied the basement level. Another family was living with friends and moved frequently as they "wore out their welcome". Jeffrey was one of my homeless students.

Jeffrey was in the 5th grade and reading at a 1st grade level. When he joined my class, our school was the 4th school he had attended in four years. He had no siblings, and he and his mother were on a waiting list for a government subsidized home located in our town. For the time being, they were living with friends.

It only took a few days for me to realize that Jeffrey's diagnosis of ADHD was completely accurate. On days when he took his medication, it generally took about an hour for it to take effect, often making the start to the day a bit chaotic. Other days, his medication was forgotten, and the entire day was chaotic, at least for Jeffrey it was.

Jeffrey was a tall, skinny boy with a careful smile who, on days when he hadn't taken his medication, seemed to be controlled by outside hands, like a crazed marionette, regardless of his efforts to do otherwise. In addition to his constant motion, he couldn't stop talking, either. He was ingenious in the ways he sought to entertain himself. He built many contraptions with erasers, pencils and a ruler. One time, his ruler became a flying projectile when his "helicopter" lost control. At least he had the forethought to yell, "Heads up!" as his ruler flew across the classroom, parting the hair of a couple of students before landing at my feet.

Often exasperated with his busyness and talkativeness, I'd say, "Jeffrey, I'm not exactly sure what to do with you." A favorite response was "Sorry you don't have a mute button to help shut me up because I don't mean to drive you crazy." Later as the year progressed, I'd often hold up an imaginary control, point it at him and mimic pushing a button. He'd laugh and do his best to be quiet for as long as he could, usually not more than a minute!

Let's fast forward to the end of the school year when Jeffrey found himself reading on grade level and completing math problems he'd never known existed. You might wonder how such a transformation occurred? I'd like to say I waved the "teaching wand" we all wish we had, and Jeffrey suddenly began to learn; however, wish as we will for such an instrument, his change didn't occur that way.

It began with a serious conversation with him about how he felt when he couldn't control his actions and words. I included his mother because, as the adult responsible for obtaining his medication, she needed to hear it from her son. He described in heartbreaking detail how he wanted to do the right things; he just couldn't seem to do it without his medication.

I worked actively with his mother to develop a trusting relationship where she understood this conversation (and the many to follow) was for the best interest of her son and certainly not a judgement about her inability to keep up with his medication. We worked together with the social worker to come up with a system for helping Jeffrey to remember to take his medication each day. When he forgot, it was agreed that Mom would be called, and she would immediately bring his medication to school. Magically, 45-minutes after taking his medication, he'd be ready to learn … and learn he did! When he could focus, he became a terrific reader and interested in sharing what he learned with others.

Mom and Jeffrey eventually moved into the house they were waiting to open up, and fortunately, it allowed for Jeffrey to continue to attend our school. In that way, he was able to feel at home in school without the stress of always starting over in a different school with new teachers and new friends.

Jeffrey is a junior in high school this year. He's no longer in the special education program, because with regular medication and a stable home environment, he is able to learn and progress without intervention. When I hear from his mother, she can't thank me enough. I tell her, "The pleasure was all mine." And that's the truth! Watching the transformation of this little boy, who worked just as hard as I did, to overcome his challenges, learn to be an advocate for himself, and surpass his wildest dreams of being a good student reminds me of why I do this job!

Did I still sometimes wish I'd had a mute button? Yep, can't lie about that. Some days were very trying indeed. However, in hindsight, Jeffrey's success couldn't have happened without his ability to describe his feelings and tell us how it felt to be him. With a mute button, his mother and I might never have known, or been able to help him.

(A portion of this story originally appeared in *Can You See Me*, 2018.)

While some might not consider "homelessness" a traumatic situation, I'd have to disagree. Home meant everything to me growing up as a child. Home was comfort, warmth, love, and a place for all my belongings. It's difficult for me to conceive my childhood and adolescence without a home to call my own.

Surprisingly, "one in 30 American children were homeless at some point last year (2013). That's about 2.5 million kids..." according to a study conducted by the National Center for Family Homelessness and reported by ABC news (https://www.nbcnews.com/business/economy/one-30-american-children-homeless-report-says-n250136). Co-author Carmela DeCandia says of homelessness, "Kids are often the collateral damage. Chronically hungry, tired and stressed, up to 40 percent of those old enough to attend school exhibit mental health issues, and they often struggle academically"

(https://www.nbcnews.com/business/economy/one-30-american-children-homeless-report-says-n250136).

Certainly, students like Jeffrey who have moved from one place to another find no comfort in the concept of home. They can't count on where they will live, nor do they have a safe place for their belongings. In addition to dealing with his ADHD, Jeffrey had to live with the fear of one day living in his mom's car. That uncertainty is more traumatizing than most can imagine for a young mind.

Great additional resources on how schools and teachers can support homeless students can be found on the U.S. Department of Education site at https:www.ed.gov/news/press-releases/education-department-releases-guidance-homeless-children-and-youth.

Belinda Adams

Thinking Outside the Box for Solutions

JAMAL: Just 5 More Minutes

I fondly remember an African American boy in my 4th grade class named Jamal. I loved that kid from the moment I laid eyes upon him. It was his quiet demeanor and slow to smile approach to life that made me realize instinctively that this was a special boy who needed a "champion" in his life.

It soon became clear that, left to his own devices, Jamal would not be making much academic growth in the 4th grade. Why you might ask? Because Jamal fell asleep. Every day. Usually for at least half of his instructional day, both in math and reading. All my efforts and my partner's efforts to engage him were to no avail.

If you've never seen it before, watching a nine-year-old fall asleep standing straight up next to your desk where he's supposed to be reading is quite a sight. I recall exactly when it happened. He was in the middle of his weekly progress monitoring when, right in the middle of a sentence, he stopped reading. Well, that wasn't completely uncommon when a student would come to a word they didn't know. So I supplied the word and encouraged him to go on. Nothing. Looking up into Jamal's face, I saw that his eyes were closed, and he was sleeping. Yep, standing straight up, he'd fallen asleep and his slack jaw and listless posture were additional proof to back up this conclusion.

Scared at first, I shook his arm, and said, "Jamal, Jamal, are you okay?" I mean, this child could be experiencing a seizure or something! Another shake of the arm, and he shook his head, and looked at me through half-mast eyes and said, "Yeah?"

"Were you sleeping?" I asked. He smiled sheepishly and said, "I guess so. Didn't I finish reading first?" With that, I sent him to his seat.

Later that day, I spoke with his math teacher and found she had been experiencing a similar situation with Jamal, although it had never happened with him standing up next to her!

Together, we decided to speak with Jamal before lunch and see why he was so tired all of the time. Jamal was not forthcoming in answering our questions, and after a few minutes, it became obvious that if we wanted answers about Jamal's overtired state, we'd have to get them elsewhere. We knew there was no point in attempting to call home because his family did not have a phone with minutes and notes sent home were not returned.

One day, I was teaching a mini-lesson about comparing fiction to historical fiction, I found my voice trailing off as I took in Jamal sitting at his desk. I couldn't help but watch as this young man, sitting erect in his chair, began to close his eyes and lean precariously to the left. I kept thinking that any minute his angled body would wake him up, but as I and the rest of the class watched in astonishment, he continued to wobble and lean further and further to the left without waking up. Finally, his buddy sitting next to him couldn't take the suspense any longer, and shook Jamal's shoulder saying "Dude, wake up! You're about to fall out of your chair." What else could I do but continue with the lesson?

Later that day, Jamal's friend, Cody, approached my partner teacher and I asked if he could talk with us. He said, "I know why Jamal is falling asleep every day in class, and I wanted to know if you wanted to know too?" Simultaneously, we answered "Yes!"

Cody explained that Jamal's bedroom wall backed up to the wall of the apartment behind him belonging to another family. It seems that the couple living there had been having some very disruptive arguments lately, and the noises of their arguing and throwing things was keeping Jamal awake at night. We thanked Cody for his honesty and genuine concern for his friend and began to think of a strategy that might help Jamal because moving certainly wasn't an option!

The next morning, while the students were immersed in their morning work, my partner teacher and I asked Jamal to step out into the hall. We told him we knew why he was falling asleep and we were very sorry to hear about the disruption seemed relieved that an adult knew of his situa

"We'd like to help you. But first, have you spoken with your Mom about what's happening?" He replied "Yes". "What did she have to say?" we prompted. He replied, "She said I could sleep on the floor in the living room or I could try sleeping with my pillow over my head, but that's all." We asked if he'd tried either of those options and he said that he'd tried the pillow thing but considering the living room already had three other sleeping occupants, he doubted that would be any better.

Trying to think quickly, I asked if he had some ear buds he could put in his ears to sleep but stopped mid-sentence as I worried about the cord becoming wrapped around his neck. My partner teacher offered to bring in ear plugs. To which he answered, "I've already tried toilet paper."

We needed additional time to think on this situation. A few days later, we explained that his sleeping in class was causing him to fall behind his peers in work. He nodded that he understood but didn't offer anything else.

Carefully, we told Jamal that on days when he fell asleep in reading (which was in the morning of each day), he would miss gym that day and take a quick "catnap" in my classroom with a beanbag, relaxing music, and the lights off. He looked at us doubtfully but seemed to know that we were not offering that as a suggestion. In that way, we explained, he'd be ready for the rest of his day, especially math in the afternoon.

For the remainder of the school year, that's the approach we took. At first, there was push back on the part of Jamal; however, after he took a few of those "catnaps" and had a better afternoon, he started to ask for them even before it was time. Fortunately, not every day!

While this strategy didn't solve the situation of Jamal's home issues, it did provide him with an opportunity to be more successful in math and reading. Further, it went a long way towards letting him know that we cared, rather than giving him punitive consequences, such as the lunch detentions, as he had received in previous years.

Jamal did make progress that year in reading and math and left headed for 5ᵗʰ grade feeling a lot

[handwritten margin note: + We don't use consequences w/ violators.]

more confidence than he was used to feeling at school.

"We have to remind ourselves, each and every day, that we don't have a window into these children's lives. ...We can't pretend we know the homes they enter once they leave us each day. While some may say these statements are not politically correct, we, educators, cannot ignore the facts or we will not find success in our classroom and neither will our students" (Adams, 2018, p. 14).

End of the Day Takeaways~

Reflecting on Jamal's situation and other situations like his that I've encountered over the years, I think we must consider our classrooms as more than places where teaching and learning takes place. If we want to have a functional classroom and students who want to be there to learn, we've got to make our classroom, their classroom, a sanctuary.

Determining how that sanctuary looks depends upon the needs of your students. For some, playing quiet, relaxing music while they work is enough to ward off thoughts of going home and facing problems. For others, like Jamal, the situation requires a more drastic course of action. Sitting with the lights off in my classroom and listening to relaxing music might be good a few times; however, it wasn't exactly the "free period" I imagined every day. But if I wanted Jamal to have the best chance of success, that was the best option available.

This, and other situations I have described, relies on one critical element to be present and that's rapport.

What does rapport look like in my classroom?

"Rapport is sensing when a student is "off" and

pulling her aside and asking if there is anything you can do.

Rapport is smiling and offering a tale of misadventure of

your own, or stories about your own children.

Rapport is being ready to stop the lesson, when needed, and

talk about feelings, empathy and the importance of

treating one another with respect.

Establishing rapport with your students will buy a

great deal of respect and hard work

from your students".

(Adams, 2018, p. 65)

"Differentiating curriculum is now a common expectation in schools, allowing students with differing learning styles to work together in the same room.

Students who present many complex challenges often need a differentiated school, where the potential in every element of the environment and curriculum is considered for its effect on student success"

(Benson, 2014, p. 167)

Wrapping Up

I'd like to leave you at the end of this book with the truth that I've learned; there are no infallible or fast strategies that can provide us with the knowledge we need to handle the unique needs of children of trauma. What I've offered within these pages are the stories of my students and the actions I took towards helping them thrive at school.

My efforts to help them achieve their goals in my classroom were sometimes a success and, other times, seemed not to matter at all. However, as a caring educator, I tried to approach each child's situation as the unique case it was and attempt to provide them with a place where they could feel safe and be emotionally available to learn.

The older the student, I believe, the more these efforts need to be a "team decision" made by you and the student. Without their "buy-in", your efforts to assist them are going to fall by the wayside. This was especially true of the 6th graders I worked with in middle school.

One important tool we can add to our toolbox is understanding and enhancing our students' resilience. The National Child Traumatic Stress Network defines resilience as "the ability of a child to recover and show early and effective adaptation following a potentially traumatic event" While some kids seem naturally born with resilience, others (especially those who are affected by trauma) suffer and have difficulty demonstrating resilience.

These are some of the students I've mentioned in this book. Remember the little boy who said, "Life is just too hard"? That's definitely a lack of resilience. As educators, we might see this lack in a variety of ways. Some things that enhance a child's resilience include:

- Developing a feeling of safety at home, school, and in the community.
- Introducing a variety of adaptive and coping skills that he or she can use in different situations
- Finding support from parents, family, school, and community.
- Locating resources that help to buffer negative consequences in their daily life.

- Helping develop a high self-esteem; an overall positive sense of self-worth.
- Assisting in feeling a sense of self-efficacy; believing he or she can be successful in different areas of life.
- Helping develop a sense of meaning in one's life, possibly including spiritual or cultural beliefs, connections with others, or goals and dreams.
- Possessing talents or skills in certain areas, such as in the arts or athletics

(http://www.nctsn.org/sites/default/files/assets/ pdfs/resilience_and_child_traumatic_stress_0 316.pdf).

Looking at this list, can you identify elements you can introduce in your classroom that could enhance resilience in your students? We've got to remind ourselves that "one size doesn't fit all" and look for ways you can enhance resilience that "fits" your teaching style and methods of classroom management. If you can't see a way to add any of these elements, it might be time to examine your teaching strategies in general. Because many of us do these things without even thinking consciously about them. My student with the pink pleather coat who practiced dancing in our classroom is an ᵔple of trying to improve her self-esteem in a

that fit with the relationship my partner teacher

_.._ I had with her.

According to Tough, what we want to create most is an "environment conducive to positive student mindsets" (Tough, 2016, p. 95). He stresses the need to establish a positive teacher/student relationship. He suggests that educators: Ask yourself, how do I treat students, how do I talk to them, how do I reward them, and how do I discipline them? He suggests we also consider our pedagogy. Ask: what do I teach, how do I teach it, and how do I assess whether my students have learned it? (Tough, 2016, p. 95). In taking this reflective approach to our instruction, we work towards creating that safe, structured learning environment that I believe all students, and especially those of trauma, are yearning for.

Children of trauma are everywhere, in every teacher's classroom, whether we are looking for them or not. I believe we have to make a conscious choice to recognize them, see their gifts and talents, and assist them in developing lifelong coping skills and strategies. Our lack of acknowledgement and support may result in students who are unruly, noncompliant, or disengaged at the least, and continuing to hurt inside at the most.

As I try to remind myself daily, these students do not come to school with the conscious intention of being unsuccessful or making the teacher feel incompetent. Although, all too often, that's the result. Benson writes in talking about strategies for the students who challenge us the most, "The moods of trauma victims can rapidly alternate between hyperarousal and numbing, and the often-uncontrollable swings significantly interrupt learning" (Benson, 2014, p. 35).

Helping these students develop strength and enhance resilience is as easy as: Developing rapport, pointing out their strengths, building competence, instilling hope, providing encouragement, looking for practical solutions, and fostering empowerment for change (Resilience and Child Traumatic Stress, www.NCTSN.org).

I ask you, "Can you be the difference for a child in trauma?"

~Challenges to Overcome~

"The ultimate goal of teaching" is developing lifelong learners. We've all heard that phrase passed around staff meetings and professional development conferences like candy.

But the real question is: How do we do it? Especially when dealing with students of trauma who may be demonstrating outward or inward behaviors that often make instructing them feel like climbing Mt. Everest every day!

Woolfolk says becoming a lifelong learner depends on becoming a "self-related learner." Her description, which includes academic learning skills and self-control explains why so many of my efforts failed to teach this concept to my students (Woolfolk, 2001, p. 10).

First, most of my students haven't yet developed academic learning skills, something I define as "knowing how to be a student". Secondly, due to the traumatic experience in their young lives and subsequent emotional issues, they haven't yet mastered self-control.

Still a work in progress …

Speaking the Unspoken

There have been so many people who have asked me if my book on trauma was going to mention or address the current trend of school shootings and school violence. I've tried, respectfully, to avoid answering the question, because I am *NOT* a political person. So, I'd like to preface this chapter with that statement again: I am NOT a political person, and as an educator, my response is based on the welfare of the children, which ultimately relates to the safety of our schools.

As an educator to a wide range of students over the years, from those in general education to those in high-need special education, from those that are so little they come to me unable to spell

names to those older students with
al/emotional issues but IQ's off the charts.
Here's what I've noticed.

Academic achievement doesn't matter when
it comes to trauma. Ability does not prevent
students from suffering from trauma. It is important
to recognize the students that are hurting from some
kind of trauma in their lives. As educators, we try to
do what we can. We recommend them to the social
worker for individual sessions. We contact parents
relentlessly about how we might partner with them
to help their child become more emotionally
available for learning. We use our special education
system to conduct extensive evaluations to assist us
in understanding the inner workings of the child's
brain. And, it goes without saying, we spend
countless hours in the classroom and out of the
classroom trying to prepare lessons that will engage
them, enlighten them, encourage them and teach
them.

Unfortunately, as we've seen from many of
the students involved in the school shootings, the
efforts of the school support system haven't been
enough to stave off the anger and resentment they

feel (for whatever the reason). It's clear to see that the trauma these children and young adults experienced that went "unseen" or "unresolved" brought them to the horrific place it did: violence.

I don't want to cast blame or throw stones at anyone or criticize the ideas that others have presented about how we might better help these students who are hurting. However, I will pose some pointed questions I've found myself asking for over 15 years while working with students of trauma.

What if schools were given budgets for more social workers so that they are not overworked, overwhelmed and often burnt out? What if the budgets that were planned to place a police officer in every school were spent instead to provide professional development for teachers and all support staff on how to address the special needs of students in trauma? What if it were mandatory for parents to follow up with recommendations from school teams that their child see a therapist? What if it were mandatory for parents to seek a Level of Care* assessment for their child when they pose a danger to themselves or others? And one step further, what if we were able to hold those parents accountable to following the suggestions of those assessments, such as family therapy and individual therapy for their child?

You see, the bottom line is, that administrators, educators and support staff cannot make significant changes in these children's lives without the financial and emotional support we so desperately need! We cannot do it alone! That's what leaves so many teachers leaving the profession due to burnout from too many years of failing to reach the students they want to reach the most. Or even worse, educators staying in the profession but no longer *feeling* the needs of her students.

You're right, I'm not addressing the politics of guns. Or the pain of shooters. Or the rights of students to feel safe at school. I am questioning our current approaches and asking, "Is there something more we can do?"

A Level of Care assessment might have different names in different areas or states. Simply stated, the social worker and school education team request a Level of Care when it is felt that the student "poses a danger to himself or others" in the school environment. This is generally due to an act of violence by the student at school or a threat he or she has made to harm himself or others. The assessment is paid for by the school district. It is an appointment with a psychologist to evaluate the child's propensity to harm himself or others. Sadly, more often than not, recommendations to seek a Level of Care are not followed through by the parents and we cannot mandate the parents to seek them for their child. Further, when parents seek a Level of Care, we have no control over whether or not the parent chooses to follow the recommendations of the assessment.

Students of all ages want to come to school and feel safe, regardless of whether they've experienced trauma themselves or seen it on TV. As violence in schools continues to rise, we can no longer afford to abandon the children who are not getting the emotional support they need. What are we, as educators, prepared to do in our classrooms, and within our schools, to make students feel safe, heal the pain they are experiencing and be available to learn?

Belinda Adams

Bibliography

Adams, Belinda. *Can you See Me? Using
     Understanding to Help Students of Poverty
     Feel Seen, Heard & Valued in the Classroom.*
     Anchor Book Press, Palatine, IL, 2018

Benson, Jeffrey. Hanging In: Strategies for Teaching
     the Students Who Challenge Us the Most.
     ASCD, Alexandria, VA, 2014.

Black, Claudia M.S.W., Ph.D. Understanding the Pain
     of Abandonment. Psychology Today, June
     2010.
     https://www.psychologytoday.com/blog/the-
     many-faces-addiction/201006/understanding-
     the-pain-abandonment

Center for Pediatric Traumatic Stress (CPTS). Medical
     Events & Traumatic Stress in Children &
     Families. No date.
     http://www.nctsnet.org/nctsn_assets/pdfs/edu_
     materials/MedicalTraumaticStress.pdf

Cevasco, Molly, Rossen, Eric and Hull, Robert. Best
     practices for supporting and educating students
     who have experienced domestic violence or
     sexual victimization. National Education
     Association, 2002-2017.
     http://www.nea.org/home/62845.htm

Child Trauma Toolkit for Educators, The National
        Child Traumatic Stress Network, October 2008.
        https://rems.ed.gov/docs/NCTSN_ChildTrauma
        ToolkitForEducators.pdf

Dockery, Karen. *When a Hug Won't Fix the Hurt*. New
        Hope Publishers, Birmingham, AL, 2000.

Hosier, David. *Child Abuse, Trauma & Recovery*,
        2015.
        https://childhoodtraumarecovery.com/tag/effect
        s-of-parentification/

Karr-Morse, Robin and Wiley, Meredith S. *Ghosts from
        the Nursery: Tracing the Roots of Violence.*
        Atlantic Monthly Press, New York, NY, 1997.*

Kauffman, James M. *Cases in Emotional and
        Behavioral Disorders in Children and Youth.*
        Pearson Education, Inc., Upper Saddle River,
        NJ, 2005.

Monahan, Cynthia. *Children and Trauma: A Guide for
        Parents and Professionals.* John Wiley and
        Sons, Inc., San Francisco, CA, 1995.

The American Academy of Experts in Traumatic
        Stress. Effects of Parental Substance Abuse on
        Children and Families, 2014.
        http://www.aaets.org/article230.htm

Tough, Paul. Helping Children Succeed, June 2016.
http://paultough.com/helping/pdf/Helping-
Children-Succeed-Paul-Tough.pdf?pdf=hcs-
pdf-landing

Vail, Priscilla L. *Emotion: the On/Off Switch for
Learning.* Modern Learning Press, Rosemont,
NJ 085556, 1994.

Woolfolk, Anita. *Educational Psychology*, Eighth
Edition, A Pearson Education Company,
Needham Heights, MA 2001.

Belinda Adams

Future Books by
Belinda Adams

Throw Away Kids

When most see those three words, it is the low-income and foster care situations that probably come to mind first. That is NOT what this book is about. Special education colleagues and diligent advocates for students with special needs, Carol Pirog and Belinda Adams, collaborate as they jump onto the slippery slope of issues plaguing students labeled as needing "special education".

Breaking protocols of what might be considered "politically correct", Carol and Belinda shed light on who these *Throw Away Kids* are and our obligation, as educators and parents, to turn the tide in their favor. *Throw Away Kids* are kids of every ethnicity and income range. They are the kids that need advocates to help them find their own voices and empower them as they move toward success.

Belinda Adams

About the Author

Belinda Adams is an elementary teacher. She has a bachelor's degree elementary education and a master's degree in special education. She has taught students in kindergarten through eighth grade. Belinda has taught general education students, students in special education, and students in regular education who needed remediation.

Belinda is the author of *Can You See Me? Using Understanding to Help Students of Poverty Feel Seen,* Heard and Valued in the Classroom. Her book is based on her experiences in the classroom. With success rates that exceed expected yearly growth, Belinda is always available to discuss solutions for those dealing with difficult students because she believes every student *wants* to learn when provided the right motivation and support. Before becoming a teacher, Belinda earned a degree in psychology, worked in the business world, and wrote a weekly editorial for a northwestern Illinois newspaper.

In her spare time, oh wait, Belinda is a teacher and an author, she doesn't have spare time. She lives in the Midwest with her husband, her son, and her dogs, Murphy & Suzy Q.

.

Belinda Adams